# an African Opera Singer

# Odyssey of an African Opera Singer

## Musa Ngqungwana

PENGUIN BOOKS

Published by Penguin Books,
an imprint of Penguin Random House South Africa (Pty) Ltd
Company Reg. No. 1953/000441/07
No 4 Estuaries, Oxbow Circle, Century Avenue, Century City, Cape Town, 7441
PO Box 1144, Cape Town, 8000, South Africa
www.penguinrandomhouse.co.za

Penguin
Random House
South Africa

First impression 2018

1 3 5 7 9 10 8 6 4 2

Publication © Penguin Books 2018
Text © Musa Ngqungwana 2018

Cover image © Paul Sirochman/The Academy of Vocal Arts
Background image: Michael Cooper/CooperShoots

All rights reserved. No part of this publication may be reproduced,
stored in a retrieval system or transmitted in any form or by any means,
either electronically, mechanically, by photocopying, sound recording or
otherwise, without the prior written permission of the copyright owners.

PUBLISHER: Marlene Fryer
MANAGING EDITOR: Ronel Richter-Herbert
EDITOR: Angela Voges
PROOFREADER: Dane Wallace
COVER AND TEXT DESIGN: Ryan Africa
TYPESETTING: Monique van den Berg/Ryan Africa

Set in 11 pt on 16 pt Minion

Printed by **novus print**, a Novus Holdings company

MIX
Paper from
responsible sources
FSC® C022948

Penguin Random House is committed to a sustainable future for
our business, our readers and our planet. This book is made
from Forest Stewardship Council ® certified paper.

ISBN 978 1 77609 297 0 (print)
ISBN 978 1 77609 298 7 (ePub)

# Contents

Author's note ..................................................................... ix

| CHAPTER 1 | Revolutionary family | 1 |
| CHAPTER 2 | Zwide township | 13 |
| CHAPTER 3 | Primary school | 27 |
| CHAPTER 4 | Dancing with the choir | 35 |
| CHAPTER 5 | High school | 47 |
| CHAPTER 6 | The Seventh-day Adventist Church | 53 |
| CHAPTER 7 | The Viola Men's Chorus | 59 |
| CHAPTER 8 | The PE Technikon Choir | 71 |
| CHAPTER 9 | Changing gears | 79 |
| CHAPTER 10 | A lucky break | 89 |
| CHAPTER 11 | Singing for Mimi Coertse | 99 |
| CHAPTER 12 | The Mother City | 109 |
| CHAPTER 13 | Opera School | 117 |
| CHAPTER 14 | The dormitory hustle | 123 |
| CHAPTER 15 | The ultimate gatecrasher | 129 |
| CHAPTER 16 | MIAGI | 141 |
| CHAPTER 17 | Valour the conqueror | 151 |
| CHAPTER 18 | The changing tides | 159 |
| CHAPTER 19 | The Academy of Vocal Arts | 167 |
| CHAPTER 20 | Battling red tape | 177 |

Postlude .......................................................................... 189
Acknowledgements ......................................................... 193

To Misiwe Dorothy Ngqungwana, my late grandmother:
*Ah Masthathu, Machisana, Ndebe, Khophoyi,
Nkomo Zibomvu, Lawu, Hasa.*

# Author's note

Having grown up in a complicated system of segregation in South Africa, then finding myself introduced to – and thriving in – an opulent art form that clashed with my impoverished upbringing, I was moved to draft a story about my unusual journey.

My book begins by exploring the effects my family felt of the political structure in South Africa, then delves into my family's life in the township, my early schooling and my initial introduction to music.

South Africa's musical traditions are rich, particularly its choral singing traditions. I found my first love of music in choirs at both school and church. I was introduced to opera through one of my choral directors, and was lucky enough to be exposed to opportunities to participate in opera performance and solo concert work, even though the path to this was not always clear. I defied the normative roles my family had set out for me while following my own path, even dropping out of engineering studies to do so.

Through the encouragement of various teachers and much study and practice, I ended up at the University of Cape Town Opera School, where I benefited from the guidance of some of the country's most learned and talented musical minds. Under their musicianship and training, I was able to earn a place at the prestigious Academy of

Vocal Arts (AVA) in Philadelphia. With additional training from the AVA, I won the Grand Finals of the Metropolitan Opera National Council Auditions in 2013, one of the greatest honours in the opera industry for a young singer. I now am grateful to be performing principal roles at leading opera houses around the United States and Europe.

I realise that not everyone is granted the opportunities I've been given and, throughout the whole process of learning my craft, I was cognisant that poverty was always at the door, and that I needed to focus as much as I could on changing my circumstances. I believe that my story, set against the unconventional background of the world of opera and turbulent South Africa, could inspire others who are working towards a dream against conditions that seem undefeatable.

# Chapter 1

# Revolutionary family

I know what poverty means, and by this I don't mean the regular struggling middle-class family or someone on welfare not having enough money to pay the electricity bill or struggling to put food on the table or milk in the refrigerator. I mean having neither a refrigerator nor the electricity to power it. I'm talking about a life where candles and Primus stoves are the power sources, and where one walks on unpaved roads, surrounded by decay and scarcity. In the world I'm referring to, winters are terrible because the shanty doesn't have proper roofing, or heating, or a ceiling. Where warm clothes don't exist to combat the easterly winds. Where health care, or even bringing home a dollar a day, is a luxury that can barely be dreamt of.

I know going to sleep without food. If there was sugar in the house, at least you could mix it with water to make 'sweet water' (*amanzi-eswekile*, as we called it). With hindsight, this was unhealthy, but at least it helped keep the hunger at bay.

I know what it's like to grow up with deprivation and depravity surrounding you because of your socio-political conditions: to look at your grandmother, the tears of pain streaming down her wrinkled, defeated and worn-out brown face, her once ever-present dimples hidden under the yoke of yearning for a better life. From the look on her face, you knew not to ask stupid questions. She had no money and no one she could ask for resources to help her survive. Prayer was all we had to get us through those days, but even that wasn't enough. Our rumbling, singing stomachs, and resulting confused minds, weren't in tune with the Holy Spirit.

I know what it's like to be homeless many times in your life. My tipping point was just after I had completed my undergraduate studies, finding myself penniless and directionless, sinking back into the depths I thought I had escaped.

But I came out of that squalid past because of grace, music, resilience and an inner drive, knowing crime would not be the answer, coupled with the help of many angels – the people who, along the way, extended their hands to me in kindness, understanding and compassion.

In this universe with its billions of stars and galaxies, there's an undisputed truth – the world is vast, and so are its possibilities. I've been in many parts of the world – traversed various continents – and I've seen the beauty in nature and in endless possibilities. I like to dream big, so when I meet folks who like to present their 'reality' and what's not 'possible', I cringe, because my experiences have given me the foresight to see past any obstacles in my way.

There are always challenges and disappointments along life's journey, but they are not what I focus on. Instead, they are lessons, returning me to the right paths and objectives. In my life, displeasures last a day, then I move on. Likewise, toxic mix-ups, fights, situations and conversations last but one day; the following day, I'm onto a new chapter.

I come from a world where small disputes can last a lifetime, and help nothing. So, I do well with people who never question my 'specious' thinking. I'd rather people judge my actions and know I live in the present. If I lived in the past, I'd be dejected and likely on drugs, living a life filled with crime, or in prison, or perhaps I'd even be dead.

Fly with me, and don't ask me where my wings are. Because, for my age, I've seen and experienced a lot, and you'll just have to have faith in that – otherwise, it may be best to stay in your own reality and let me float in my own dreams. I've always known I was different. Borrowing the words of former president of South Africa Thabo Mbeki, 'I am an African. I owe my being to the hills and the valleys, the mountains and the glades ...' I'm a free spirit, hovering through nature, unrestricted. When I fall, I get up.

But I am getting ahead of myself! My friends call me Chief or Musa. I was born on a rainy Tuesday morning on 31 July 1984, in Port Elizabeth, South Africa. My home town is in the Eastern Cape province, over 750 kilometres east of Cape Town. Port Elizabeth is one of South Africa's major ports and has a population of nearly 1.3 million. British settlers founded the city in 1820, and the city provided housing for them, strengthening the boundary region between the Cape Colony and the Xhosa people.

My mother's uncle, Phumlani Ngqungwana, christened me Bayempini, a name derived from the Zulu word *impi*, which means 'war'. Thus, Bayempini means 'they have gone to war'. One might ask why I was named after such a hostile sentiment. However, my name was inspired by my mother's uncles, all of whom were members of the African National Congress (ANC), then viewed as communist rebels. The ANC was banned as a political party in South Africa in early 1960, but it functioned covertly in the years that followed. My name defines the state of its members' resolve as they planned their *coup d'état* through guerrilla warfare.

So, I was born into a political family whose norms and philosophies defined my early childhood. My mother, who is of Zulu heritage from her father's side, tried to balance the weight of this masculinity with Musawenkosi, a Zulu word meaning 'God's grace'. I always thought this name gave me clemency, should I need it, and the sensitivity I've carried with me throughout my life.

My birth year was, on the socio-political front, a very difficult time in South Africa. The period marked the rise of violent protests known as the Township Uprising. These resulted from many factors, including the establishment of the Tricameral Parliament, divided into the House of Assembly, House of Representatives and House of Delegates. This new parliamentary format included limited representation for coloured and Indian people, but it left out black people.

As expected, many black political parties opposed these reforms and argued that this further exclusion of black Africans in state affairs would aggravate the tensions that already existed. Black Africans lobbied for the inclusion of a Bill of Rights, which would protect individual freedoms against state misuse. My life began amid this complicated racial situation, which had, at its roots, segregation and apartheid philosophies.

When I was ten months old, intelligence operatives set fire to our house in the middle of the night. The perpetrators had come looking for my mother's uncle, Phumlani Ngqungwana, on orders to apprehend him.

My grandmother recalled that they came just after 11 p.m. For the rest of her life, she never went to bed until after that time.

'My son, that was a very difficult night, but God is always with us,' she explained to me when I was older, as tears ran down her wrinkled cheeks. She continued: 'Just after 11 p.m., while we were all sound asleep, the perpetrators caught us unawares. We heard shouts – "Phumlani, you dog, where are you hiding? Come out! We are waiting for you!" No response came from the house. Their rage built.

My mother, your great-grandmother, Malo, was still alive, and she instructed everyone to keep quiet. The house was full of women and young children, including you, Musa. Your mother breastfed you to stop you from crying at the sound of the banging on our doors. Malo said soft prayers, hoping that something would discourage the thugs.

'One of them, carrying a double axe, went to the shanty at the back of the house where Phumlani usually slept and bashed the wooden door down. Phumlani wasn't there; someone had tipped him off so he could break free ahead of time. We hoped that, since he wasn't there, the agents would leave us alone. But instead, they still attacked, thinking we were shielding him inside the house.

'The perpetrators surrounded the house, smearing a chemical substance on the doors. We were dumbfounded about what was happening outside, as it had gone quiet. Then, the agents lit the substance. Smoke entered our rooms, and the house went up in flames. As we ran to open the doors, whatever chemical they had put on the doors stoked the fire, making opening them impossible.

'With flames outside licking the night sky, our screams inside alerted the neighbours, who rushed in to help, breaking the windows to help us escape. Your mother wrapped you in her arms to protect you, but had no way to put out the embers that alighted on her head and began slowly eating away at her hair. The fire burned off her hair and damaged her scalp, causing her to use wigs and hair extensions for the rest of her life. I had an asthma attack because of the chemical substance the thugs used.'

As my grandmother finished telling me the story, she was overcome with emotion from reliving the incident. I gave her a long embrace; even though I didn't understand her predicament, I could feel her pain.

I was the only one who came out of the ordeal unscathed. That nothing hurt me, I believe to this day, was only because of God's grace and favour.

This incident displaced us for over two years while the municipality rebuilt the house, and we went to live at the home of Koko Ngqungwana, one of my grandmother's brothers. I have no memories of him, as he passed away while I was still young, not long after the fire.

I asked my grandmother why government agents would go to such extreme lengths to get to Phumlani. She explained that Phumlani was involved with Umkhonto we Sizwe (MK) underground operations. Along with many other cadres, he carried out MK orders. These orders traced their history back to 1979, when the ANC executed armed operations through a special operations unit that focused on high-impact attacks on strategically placed military and economic targets, which they deemed were in support of the ruling regime.

The rationale behind this was that the attacks would improve the morale of the oppressed and unfavourably impact the economic sustainability of the apartheid system. MK's bigger vision was to wage an unrelenting armed struggle within South Africa, in small teams across strategic positions in the country. All the comrades known to be part of these operations, like Phumlani, were sought by the ruling government.

Government agencies were also notorious for kidnapping suspects, who would then disappear under the Terrorism Act. The Act allowed someone suspected of involvement with terrorism – which was very sketchily defined as anything that may 'endanger the maintenance of law and order' – to be detained for sixty days without trial. There was no obligation to release information about these detainees; often, their families would never see them again.

There are countless stories of atrocities arising from the Act. I suspect, had the government operatives found my mother's uncle that night, that a similar fate would have befallen him. Phumlani was to fall victim to this Act later when the authorities arrested him on his way to Lesotho and incarcerated him in the infamous Robben Island Maximum Security Prison. Phumlani's brother, Lizo 'Bright' Ngqungwana, was also held there. Lizo was also part of the MK's underground network. He was arrested in Cape Town on 12 August 1987 and sentenced to life imprisonment in a case that became known as *State v. Ngqungwana and 14 others*.

When the government liberated political prisoners after Nelson Mandela's release, Lizo served in the new South African National Defence Force as a high-ranking officer until his untimely death in 1998 in a car accident. Of the original fourteen who stood trial with him, one other comrade has also since died.

I remember when my grandmother took Phumlani's daughter, Senzeni, and me on trips to visit the political prisoners in our family. Our first trip was to 'Rooi Hell' Prison in Port Elizabeth, now called Port Elizabeth Correctional Centre, to see Phumlani. I remember the big walls and gates, and how the armed guards would move around to observe the prisoners and listen to their conversations.

'These guards think we have come here to discuss confidential information about the struggle in this prison. They are deranged,' my grandmother remarked.

When they transferred Phumlani to Robben Island, the three of us went to visit him there.

We took the Translux bus, which in those days was a luxury coach that travelled for twelve hours through the night, with some stops between Port Elizabeth and Cape Town. Since we couldn't possibly afford such a trip, the South African Council of Churches (SACC) and the South African Red Cross Society provided us with funds to make this journey, as they did for other families of political prisoners. My grandmother gave us the backgrounds of the cities we passed along the coastal route via Humansdorp, Jeffreys Bay, Knysna, George, Mossel Bay and Stellenbosch.

We reached Cape Town at about seven in the morning. On our arrival, we took a taxi to Cowley House, an old house in Chapel Street in Woodstock owned by the SACC, where all these families like mine used to stay on their way to see their loved ones. As scheduled, we took a transport to the dock, where a boat ferried us to Robben Island. The ferry trip took a good forty minutes.

This was one of my favourite parts of the journey, perhaps because my grandmother did not like it. She was afraid of the waves and we learnt she was seasick; she asked what would happen if we drowned. She also asked in amazement why I did not seem afraid of the water, while covering her face and hanging on for dear life each time the ferry hit a big wave and pitched sideways.

She asked whether the waves made me dizzy. My answer was always a 'no' and a laugh.

As we approached Robben Island, where the ferry docked not far from the prison, my grandmother grabbed my hand and held it tightly. I may have teased my grandmother about her fear on the boat ride, but when we got to the gates of the prison, the three of us could sense we were in a different, and harsh, environment – one in which no human deserved to be locked up. At the entrance, a big sign stood on top of a bridge-like layout. Underneath it was a gateway, and it was supported on each side by a grey stone structure.

On the sign, written vertically on the extreme left and right, was 'Welcome' and the Afrikaans '*Welkom*'. Horizontally, on the top of the sign, was written 'Robben Island' and, right beneath it, dead centre, 'We Serve with Pride' – and the Afrikaans equivalent, '*Ons*

*Dien Met Trots'*. And then, on each side of this maxim, there were two signs: on the left, an emblem with what looked like an open book beneath the scales of justice, and on the right, the flower of an arum lily.

My grandmother shook her head as soon as she saw the sign. 'We serve with pride, my foot, those devils incarnate,' she muttered, stopping just short of spitting and cursing the ground on which her spit fell. High walls and armed guards surrounded the place, keeping watch at all hours of the day and night. The visitors' centre was just to the right of the entrance. This ensured that we could not access the prison and witness the immense immorality of those prison cells.

I feared for my life, but my grandmother, though frightened herself, comforted me: 'Don't worry, my child, all will be well.'

We were instructed that we could sit and talk to my uncles, but we had to keep our distance: no physical contact. The prisoners were allowed one visit every six months; we had a maximum of thirty minutes. The prison officials insisted that the conversations be only in English or Afrikaans – no native languages were allowed, for fear of covert information being exchanged.

Even though I was young, on seeing Lizo and Phumlani in these surroundings – trapped, wearing numbered prison clothes – I could sense that evil ruled that place. My grandmother tried to cheer us up and bring some joy, but she, too, was overwhelmed by anger and fear. The last of those trips was in 1991; after the government released Nelson Mandela in 1990, they freed most other political prisoners too. However, there are still some – whom they transferred to prisons like Pollsmoor, and who represented parties like the Pan Africanist Congress (PAC) – who've yet to taste freedom.

As I reflect on it, it is a tribute to the human spirit that any of those men survived and could rejoin society after the fall of the apartheid government. I am lucky to have had my grandmother raise me until I went to college and share these family journeys with me and teach me the value of our heritage and history.

My grandmother was a very strong woman. Misiwe, her first name, derives from the Xhosa word *ukumisa*, which means 'to build upon'. Her mother, Malo, had an unfortunate number of miscarriages and lost two babies. The story goes that Malo and her husband, the late Reverend Milani Ngqungwana of the Presbyterian Church, known in Xhosa as *Rhabe*, both came from farms around Somerset East in what was then the eastern part of the Cape Province.

Upon learning that Malo was pregnant again, they became anxious lest the same thing happen. However, this time my grandmother was born – a healthy baby who lived to be nearly seventy years old. They christened her Misiwe, the foundation of the family they were to build upon. The couple had five more healthy children before their untimely separation, for reasons I don't know. The Reverend had seven more children when he remarried.

Thus, when I was born, my great-grandmother and grandmother raised me. My granny, like her mother, had marriage misfortunes, in Ladysmith, a city about 250 kilometres north-west of Durban, where my mother was born. When Malo fell ill in Port Elizabeth, my grandmother had an added incentive to return to Port Elizabeth. She brought the kids with her – my mother, her younger sister and her two brothers.

My grandmother was a very superstitious woman. For instance, she did not want us to watch TV during lightning storms, which were common in my home town during the summer. She feared that the lightning would somehow come into the house, and that it was a bad omen to watch television during those 'ordeals'.

I need not tell you that we bumped heads when it so happened that the storms coincided with my favourite TV show; I would not allow anyone to switch off the TV.

'Hey, you, daredevil child, switch off that TV! There are lightning storms outside and they will burn you,' my grandmother would berate me. I would comply, only to turn it back on when she fell asleep, even if it meant keeping the volume low.

I spent a lot of time with her, from when I was a baby through to my high-school years, when I started to crave independence. Much of that time I spent in the kitchen, as she loved baking. One of my favourite things was the breakfast cereal we call pap – a traditional porridge made from maize meal, mixed with a little bit of butter or milk.

Another favourite was *umdoko* or *amarhewu* – a traditional non-alcoholic, fermented, nutritious beverage with a distinctive sour flavour. I would add a little bit of sugar and drink it in one gulp. And another favourite was steamed bread. I can tell you, I have travelled the world, and I am perhaps biased, but no steamed bread I have ever eaten since matches my grandmother's recipe. At times, I mixed the steamed bread with *maasbanker* (horse mackerel), hake or snoek, especially on Saturdays, as my grandmother loved cooking fish on weekends.

My grandmother also loved cooking *umngqusho* or samp, a dish with several variants but made primarily of *stampmielies* (coarsely crushed corn, cooked with sugar beans). Misiwe would add butter, onions and potatoes and let them simmer; she often mixed this with sausages or red meat to make a stew.

I never did learn to cook: instead of learning from her as she prepared our food, I would steal samples of my favourites while waiting for meals. 'Devil of a child, go watch TV instead of finishing the food in this kitchen!' she would say. I just couldn't stop.

# Chapter 2

# Zwide township

Despite my grandmother's love and care, I grew up an angry child, hostile to my father and to any male authority figure I perceived as disingenuous. Being baptised and raised in the polarising, measurable harm of single parenthood in the township made me question whether my father ever loved me or whether his self-indulgence was more important to him. Whatever may have happened between my parents did not justify my father's absence from my life.

I cut him out of my heart and mind, not caring what his reasons were. There was no way he could make amends for all those lost years.

In my youth, I loathed my father, but as I matured, I realised that my anger would exhaust my energy and would only hurt me. I stopped dwelling on what could have been and focused on what was at hand. Thanks to the support and love I received, especially from my grandmother, I channelled and let go of that anger.

My grandmother raised me because my mother had had me out of wedlock when she was twenty years old. It was not uncommon for grandparents to raise their grandchildren. I was fortunate enough that Malo was still alive when I was born, and that two experienced and loving women raised me.

I remember Malo taking me with her to collect her pension cheques, and putting biscuits and sandwiches in her handbag for me whenever she took me with her to run an errand. I do not know when she passed away; I was still young. But a week after we laid her to rest, I was playing in the backyard when I heard my grandmother exclaim, 'Gracious God, Musa, come in here, my son!'

I ran inside, and there was my grandmother with Malo's handbag.

'Look at what was in Malo's handbag, would you?'

I peeked into the bag. There, waiting for me to find them, were two ginger and raisin biscuits she had tucked away for me.

'Can I eat them now? Please?' I pleaded.

Grandmother, smiling, said, 'Here you go, my son. Remember this moment, and how your great-grandmother loved you.'

I had tremendous support at home from these loving women, but I always felt that something was missing. Following an instinctive need to identify with my own gender, I kept trying to find a masculine role model outside the house in my neighbourhood. The intermittent presence of the men from my mother's family, who lived elsewhere, was not enough.

I replaced my missing father with older boys in the township and learnt male conduct through trial and error – by imitating what I saw, rather than being taught by a loving father. I wanted the neighbourhood boys to accept me. These older lads imparted misguided information and training to me because they had no positive father figures either; they did not know what it is to be a man themselves. The whole picture was a skewed one that overemphasised machismo and ignored the responsibilities that men need to bear in the community.

Looking back on those early years, I cannot help but think we wasted our free time because none of us had father figures to help us shape it into productive patterns. This made it easy for older boys to sway us younger boys and lead us down the wrong path.

The weekends were a time of both excitement and anxiety for all us younger lads. We were elated to be free from the bonds and strict structure of school, and we could play soccer and touch rugby to our hearts' content; but weekends were also reminders of the hierarchical order in which the older lads pitted us against one another for sport and amusement, all under the guise of making us stronger.

On one such weekend, Bhiza, one of the older lads, lectured me: 'It is a tough world we live in! You must know how to defend yourself and earn respect. Township life is not for sissies. You're not afraid, are you, Musa?'

With a knowing look in his eye, he nodded and pointed to young Makhosonke, my pal, whom we called Popeye after the cartoon character of the same name, since he was so tall and thin. However, Makhosonke needed no fortifying spinach: Popeye needed to fight. He could hold his own.

To please my general and gain 'respect', I charged at Popeye like an enraged bull. Expecting my move, Makhosonke quickly swerved to the left, leaving his right foot wilfully in my path, just enough to cause me to trip and taste the salt of the earth. He then jumped in for a brawl on the ground, which was a miscalculation on his part: he had now lost his upper hand, as I was much stronger than he was. We wrestled and butted heads until I cut him just an inch above his left brow. As he bled on my T-shirt, I worried that I had injured him badly, but it was only a small cut. While I was in repose mode, a rookie move on my part, he picked up grass and force-fed it to me, then stood up and quickly ran for cover.

I may have been the victor, but Popeye was wittier. The grass move was ingenious, and I was mad and embarrassed. All the boys were laughing at me, particularly the older ones.

That was our ritual: fighting all the time, whether we liked it or not. Our physical actions trumped our verbal means of communication, hindering our abilities to solve problems rationally.

We had no sense of the long-term ramifications of our behaviour. We did not know how to address our feelings or understand the fuller implications of masculinity, so we could not liberate ourselves from this yoke of machismo, which limited our interactions with women.

This became more evident when we chatted with girls – or tried to. They always seemed well advanced, ahead of us with their emotional maturity. I couldn't communicate how I felt, and it was easier to deal with boys because I could punch them or use strong language to get my message across, but with girls, I realised that wouldn't do and it frustrated me that the only acceptable social norm – proper communication – was lacking in me.

When I liked a girl, I found it hard to express myself and felt very disappointed when my affections weren't reciprocated. It hadn't dawned on me that I scared them with my forceful, brash tone. I remember feeling ready to have a girlfriend when I was ten or eleven (if this type of relationship could be classified as such at this young age; then again, our situation was unique in the township – we grew up fast). The influence of the older boys baptised us into the themes of adulthood before we were ready.

Nomaphelo lived on the next street over from mine. Her father was short and brawny, a mechanic infamous for his temper who didn't shy away from throwing his tools, or any car parts he could lift, to get his message across. Nomaphelo had three older brothers, including one who was only four or five years older than me. He loved fighting and could back up his tough words with every fibre of his body. Her sisters, likewise, were neither dumb nor pushovers; it's safe to say that one messed with this family at his or her own peril.

## ZWIDE TOWNSHIP

But still, I liked this girl; my machismo got in the way of reason when I wanted something. Any other rational person would have steered clear of this situation, but I let my emotions take the lead.

It was a Saturday afternoon, after one of my regular brawl sessions with my comrades. I don't recall whom I had fought, but we were now just sitting on a street corner close to a local shop, smoking Lexington cigarettes, talking trash and discussing what every 'hood boy aspired to be – a big gangster with money and a flock of women. We didn't have to imagine this, because our township, like all others, had plenty of such gentlemen. We liked a gangster called Vleis (Afrikaans for 'meat'), who stood at an imposing 201 centimetres and must have weighed no fewer than 100 kilograms. He robbed others at his own will, and he scared the adults, but we worshipped him because he had plenty of girlfriends and a following of lieutenants who would do his bidding – including stabbing others for him. The money came easily to him; he dressed well and loved spending his money at our local shebeens. In our convoluted reasoning, we thought he had quite the life – even two years later, when the police shot and killed him.

As we were mired in our adolescent folly, in my peripheral vision I saw a girl approaching us from across the street. It was Nomaphelo, and she was beautiful; I was simply smitten.

'She's mine!' I bellowed.

'Go for it, mate,' said Bhiza. I was lucky: she was too young for the older lads, as she was about the same age as me and Popeye, and Popeye wasn't interested in challenging me on this one.

I stood up from the unpaved road we were sitting on and approached her with a fake swagger, trying to imitate the other gangsters – who I swore were hunchbacks because they never walked straight.

'Nomaphelo, come here, baby,' I hollered.

'Who told you my name? How do you know me?' she retorted.

'That's beside the point. Come here – I want to talk to you!'

'No, I can't. I'm running errands and my father would be upset if I were late or spoke to boys on the street,' she taunted back.

'Your old man is not here, is he? Come here before you piss me off!'

Like a meek sheep heading for slaughter, she came. I took her by the arm. My grip must have been too tight – she flinched, but I didn't let go.

'Look, baby, I like you. How about you be my girl?'

As soon as she could untangle herself from my grasp, she ran away.

It only dawned on me later the trouble I had potentially got myself into. If it weren't for Bhiza's protection, Nomaphelo's brother would have had me for lunch. He wanted my blood, and I had to apologise and promise not to bother his sister again. Bhiza also lied for me, telling him the incident hadn't been that bad and that Nomaphelo must have exaggerated it. But, for a good month – which seemed like an eternity – I didn't walk down their street and avoided wherever I thought her brother might be until the dust had settled.

When I listened to reason and my senses, I knew I needed help to address this inherent problem, but it would take a long time before I matured.

And thus began my search for a deeper understanding of the kernel of township life and better ways to contribute to the re-emergence of our old ways: the spirit of *ubuntu*, human kindness, and what it means to be a black man in society.

South Africa's townships were built, mostly, between the late nineteenth century and the end of apartheid, in urban living areas reserved for non-whites. The communities in these townships faced many troubling issues. Most often, the homes were on land owned not by the occupying families but by wealthy landlords, corporations or the government.

Many families were migrants who came from rural areas, small towns and the former Bantustans into which the apartheid government had pushed them. They came to the big cities in search of jobs, with meagre ways of supporting themselves and no place to stay. As a desperate measure, they built squatter camps on plots not allocated to them through the proper channels. These families always faced chances of eviction by the government.

At home, we did not have electricity until I was eleven years old; we used Primus stoves for cooking and a car battery to power the TV. Still, we had clean water and access to municipal services, despite living in a squalid house that had two bedrooms, a small kitchen and a dining room that also served as a living room. To meet the housing demand, each township house had a shack or two made of wood in its backyard. In addition, those families who had money built extensions or real flats in their backyards.

It is an interesting phenomenon to assess. As the older brothers or uncles came of age and started their own families, instead of leaving home, they built their own flats in the backyard, resulting in six or more people living in one household – which, most of the time, had only one or two people who were employed.

Our mothers needed to work a lot of the time; most of the children from the township were left alone, often in the supposed care of their unemployed uncles or neighbours, who were often irresponsible, focused on their own perils and stresses, or not equipped to deal with children.

You may ask why township parents did not send their children to day care. They simply could not afford it, relying on their relatives at home to take care of the children while they went to work out of need. Their rationale was that if they were the breadwinners, the least the relatives could do was look after the children.

Poverty demeans the mind. Daily priorities may differ from person to person, or from home to home, but the negative impact of poverty is always present. The many dimensions of poverty shape people's lives. Most obvious is the lack of work opportunities in people's quest to earn a living wage. This affects people in different ways; their priorities shift, becoming less healthy. Alcohol and substance abuse is a common way in which some people deal with their problems. We all know what substance abuse does to a person's brain and how it debases common sense and prudence. Now think about that same person as the one who looks after his sister's child.

The effects of poverty on children's development can lead to aggressive behaviours that protect them psychologically against their unsympathetic environment. Many children who don't receive proper care at home develop behavioural problems at school, which can lead to their expulsion or them dropping out. I was fortunate to have liked school and not to have let my conditions at home affect my progress. My grandmother was very strict and would let heaven and earth collide before she saw my schoolwork suffer.

The lack of education further burdens the families in these neighbourhoods, as does the lack of access to health care and other aspects of social infrastructure, including housing and credit facilities. Let me argue then that without access to quality education, health care and income-earning opportunities, the lives of these folks are a daily struggle just to survive.

Most of the men did not stand on the sidelines; although they cared about finding employment, they had given up on their quest after one too many trials in the workforce or rejection letters from companies. Some of the men had worked for years but had lost their jobs and taken a beating because of it. Political volatility and the withdrawal of international companies during the apartheid years led to substantial joblessness; when I was growing up, at least 72 per cent of the black population in my home town lived below the poverty line. There were far too many people seeking far too few jobs.

My home town had a large trading and manufacturing sector, which, for many years, had attracted people from the rural parts of the country. Port Elizabeth forms part of what is today the Eastern Cape province, one of the poorest provinces in the country.

The withdrawal of giant companies such as General Motors from Port Elizabeth, in which thousands of people lost employment, dropped many into the jobless hole. When you factor in that poverty in households headed by women, like my childhood home, is higher in comparison to the general population because women continue to earn less than men, you realise that the households where men had been laid off were left to the care of the very women who earned less, on average, than men.

Gangs offered a seemingly appealing way out of this poverty cycle. After all, the meagre salaries earned by our single mothers could not hold up to the 'easy' money won by a life of crime. However, no one spoke about the consequences that accompanied these criminal activities, and that this easy money came at its own price.

I know that most of us consistently found making ethical decisions problematic, such as whether to feel guilty after we'd been disobedient and accept the blame, or to refuse to take responsibility.

One day, when I was about twelve, a couple of my gang friends and I encountered a drunk man who lived in our neighbourhood. He did not know us particularly well, but thought we were honest kids from the neighbourhood, so he gave us money to go and buy him some brandy from the local tavern. He had run out and had seen us playing rugby on our street.

We took the money and went to the tavern as instructed, but, on our way there, one of my older friends commented, 'That old man is drunk and will never know who took his money and ran away with it!'

Without further thought, we split the money evenly. When he realised we had robbed him, he apparently cursed us – but, in his drunken state, he couldn't remember who had done it. I knew it was wrong to have stolen his money, but I did it because I wanted to belong to the gang and succumbed to the pressure. Our crime may not have been hefty, but it was wrong nonetheless.

Growing up, I was surrounded by friends who lived on the same street. Single mothers or grandparents raised all of us, barring three. Furthermore, we all had a bunch of much older uncles still living at home with their mothers.

All our families lived from pay cheque to pay cheque. Most of our mothers or grandmothers worked in factories or as domestic workers, taking care of affluent families in the suburbs. To get there, they took buses or minibus taxis in the early hours of the morning, then slaved away for hours. After putting in a full day's work, they would return in the evenings to prepare dinner for their families. Each hard-working woman fed children and a bunch of old men, who were often unwilling to put in the effort to find work.

Our house was no exception to being overcrowded with people. Before I started preparatory school, which was just under two kilometres from my house, my grandmother's cousin, Thembi Ngqungwana, joined us. He was in his late forties when he came to live with us, a divorcee whose children lived in New Brighton township, about three and a half kilometres from Zwide township.

## ZWIDE TOWNSHIP

Thembi was unemployed, having lost his job at General Motors. So, he also became dependent on my grandmother's meagre salary. He seemed to have lost the will to fight and reclaim his life, and you could tell that drinking continued to chip away at his sensibilities. Sometimes he talked to himself, mumbled, or complained about nothing. He was very talkative and full of ideas that never came to fruition. Always defensive when someone suggested he look for a job, he would come up with a litany of excuses. I never understood his refusal to seek work opportunities.

Even though Thembi loved drinking, to his credit he was neither a troublemaker nor disrespectful to anyone. He took good care of his looks, remembering the days when he used to work. He had immense knowledge about celebrity gossip and politicians; he could write a book about the stories that interested him. If only he could have directed that same energy at important things, such as finding a job using the knowledge and tools he had at his disposal.

Perhaps it is unfair to have expected that much from him. Not everyone thinks and reacts the same way to issues, and I could not have understood his life and what he had been through.

During weekdays, I saw little of him, as I was always at school. On weekends, the entertainment started.

'Hey, Bomza,' he would call to me, 'how do I look?'

He would pat my head but never ask me how my day had been.

Then, he would sit down, eating more than his share of the food set out on the table. Afterwards, he would head out, walking with a swagger, as if he were some important guy in the township with somewhere pressing to be. I waved goodbye, knowing we wouldn't see him again until he came staggering home in the wee hours of the morning.

One thing that puzzles me to this day is that so many poor people lack the means to support their families or themselves but never want for alcohol. Somehow, whenever my uncle visited the shebeens, there were kindred spirits willing to share their beers or cocktails with him. Township life is communal. There is no drinking alone and enjoying privacy – your friends or neighbours will jump at the opportunity to take advantage of you.

In the township milieu, we had many shebeens that were an alternative to the pubs and bars in the central business districts and suburbs – residential areas where Africans could not live. Women, whom we knew as Shebeen Queens, ran them. This was not a remarkable scene, but one that was in congruence with the ancient African tradition of women, not men, having the role of brewing alcohol.

The Shebeen Queens sold home-brewed and distilled alcohol and provided patrons with a place to meet and discuss political and social issues. As with all things illegal, the police were on the lookout to arrest patrons and owners during segregation. It is interesting to note that, when the shebeen owners returned from jail, they would set about reopening the business, defying the system – a nod to the importance of the shebeens in unifying the community and providing safe havens for political discussions. The shebeens also provided a space for music by local and international artists who opposed segregation.

By the time my grandmother's cousin had come to live with us, most shebeens had become legal, owing to the political changes in our country. Thembi loved going to a place called Qhebo's, owned by an eccentric woman. He would also go to places such as Joe's Tavern or Oom Cola's Tavern, but the other places he frequented were dodgy.

Thembi got intoxicated every weekend on his favourites, Castle Lager or brandy. He and his band of shebeen drunks would go out and then come home in the early hours of the morning, singing church hymns in an off-key and intrusive manner to those just trying to catch up on their sleep after a hard week's work.

'We are on the path to the land of righteousness, a home to people who live in peace,' Thembi sang as he staggered into the house one evening.

'Thembi!' Grandmother bellowed. 'Have you no manners, waking us up in the middle of the night with this noise? You sing about God when you do not know where the church doors are. You have no shame, and I am sick and tired of your behaviour!'

Thembi apologised: 'Pardon me, my big sister who takes care of me! I shan't do it again,' only to continue the cycle the following weekend.

This grown man had the audacity to acknowledge that someone was taking care of him at his age and then continue his poor behaviour, which I witnessed again and again. Even when I was young, the situation made me angry; I wondered why an able-bodied man with adequate manual-labour skills couldn't look for a job.

It was all a mystery. I did not comprehend how dysfunctional we all were as a family unit – nor could I measure the dysfunction of my neighbourhood. My friends and I all thought that poverty, growing up in these conditions, was normal, and that it was the way God had designed the world, and that we should accept and abide by it. I now understand that there was nothing commendable about those conditions. They are below the standard of human dignity.

# Chapter 3

# Primary school

I remember little about primary school – Mnqophiso Lower Primary School, where I did Grades 1 to 4. There was nothing of consequence about it, except for learning my ABCs. But I do remember the first day of school. In fact, the night before, my grandmother, the chief director of morning operations, systematised everything. She ironed my school clothes, prepared lunch and figured out the other necessities. In the year preceding my Grade 1 year, she had already tried to stock up on all the essentials in bulk whenever she could, so that, for each season of the year, I could have proper school attire.

On the morning of that first day of school, she woke me up very early, to which I did not take kindly: I am not a morning person. I also did not understand why going to school was such a big deal. If all I could do was eat my delectable foods, play and sleep, that would've sufficed. But no, she had other plans for my future.

'Wake up, my child, it's time for school! If you want to become a famous doctor, then you must study.'

She restated the importance of education and its investment while I mumbled gibberish to no avail, still groggy from sleep. By persuasion or force, my grandmother would ensure I woke up. Our home was not egalitarian. She ruled with love, but did not spare me her wet kitchen cloth if I misbehaved.

It was her ritual to pray with me before going to bed and before I left for school. The night prayer session was longer, much to my dislike and impatience: we would kneel, and it would feel like forever. She took her time, praying for her family and calling each one by name. The prayer ended with the Lord's Prayer in our native language, recited like a high priest leading a prayer from the Ark of the Covenant. I was her young disciple, reciting after her. Next to the lamp on the table beside the bed was a wet cloth placed on a saucer, ready to deal with the young priest-in-training in case I protested the kneeling part.

While I loathed those moments, and there are too many to recount, I now realise the love and wisdom of my grandmother's teaching me discipline. She gave me the gift of prayer – of aligning my thoughts with God. Though she had not attended church for some time – she hated the political infighting for positions in her congregation, yet she would not go to another church – she was a woman of faith. Her prayers were full of conviction and gave me a blessed assurance that, before I set out for school every day, everything would be okay and I would be sheltered under God's wings.

I later realised the importance of those sessions, especially when life was hard. I recall one of her favourite hymns, which also, apparently, was one of her father's favourites – a Methodist hymn she sang in difficult times to gather her strength:

God, you are with your people always.
Keeping and helping them in all places.
You are with them when they cross rivers, facing illuminating fires, you are with them.
In persecution, you will strengthen them.

Amid dangers, even, you have kept them.
As your people, they look up to you Lord; as your people, they thank and trust you.

What I also remember about my preparatory school is my class teacher, Mrs Ngqwarhu. She must have been in her early forties. She was a strong and stern type, much like my grandmother. In those days, teachers still practised corporal punishment. She did not spare us her baton when we misbehaved or talked back to her.

She often asked us the universal question: 'What do you want to be when you grow up?'

My reply was always the same. 'I want to be a lawyer or a doctor.'

Mrs Ngqwarhu would throw a rod or chalkboard duster in your direction if you were uncertain about your future employment prospects. She pushed us to have big dreams and had a resolve to teach us the basics as best she could in our native language. Few of us ever dared to report her to the principal or our parents or guardians.

Through her discipline and guidance – and that of another teacher, Ms Maninjwa – I completed Grade 4 at the top of my class with an A+ average, something that always brought rewards at home. I studied hard because I always looked forward to those rewards. Poor as we were, there was always something special at the end of the year, no matter how small. In my soul, these rewards were significant, and I knew they came from the heart.

As part of my reward, my grandmother would save up during the year so I could travel with her to see her siblings who lived across the country. This afforded me opportunities to see our vast country and its sheer beauty. Another great reward was an emotional one, seeing how proud my grandmother was of how smart I was, boasting about my academic achievements to her family. Every December, when I visited her siblings, I knew I would get new clothes for school, and a pair or two of jeans, or pants for church.

I was ready to move into Grade 5. I applied for a place at Isaac Booi Senior Primary School. It was a great public school, with quality education and stringent entry requirements. That December holiday, I visited another of my grandmother's sisters, MaNozi (short for Ms Nozizwe). She lived in Keiskammahoek, a small village on the slopes of the Amatola Mountains just under 50 kilometres from King William's Town, at the meeting of the Gxulu and Keiskamma rivers. The city's native name, Qoboqobo, means 'a delicate item'; it is a sheltered spot.

MaNozi was a staff nurse in a local clinic. She is a lovely person, and I enjoyed visiting her home, as she always spoiled me with good food and the freedom to roam around her big house, or I could watch movies. In my native Xhosa, of her we would say '*unobubele*' – that she was a charitable person. Taking a tour of her home and the surrounding countryside afforded me an opportunity to experience life outside of our destitute ways.

One day, on our way back home, she suggested that we visit King William's Town, which is near Bhisho, the capital of what is today the Eastern Cape province.

As we passed rows of beautiful houses, she explained: 'In these houses dwell government officials and affluent and educated people. If you stay at school and commit to furthering your education, you will one day own a house and beautiful car just like these.'

Skuvethi (my grandmother's nickname) and I returned home in time for Christmas with gifts and new clothes, including a new school uniform, to start the year. Summertime, starting in December, was always one of my favourite times of the year. My grandmother and her daughters, including my mother, created miracles every Christmas. It was our version of America's Thanksgiving – we always had plenty and wanted for nothing. Surrounded by these maternal figures, I learnt the value of gratitude from a young age.

I remember Skuvethi carrying on her parents' tradition by waking us up at five in the morning to pray and give thanks for all the blessings of the year, her family members, and health and prosperity.

'Time to get up!'

I heard her voice and groaned, burying my head under the pillow for a few more minutes of sleep.

Then I remembered the wet cloth and that it was Christmas and tumbled out of bed, throwing on some clothes and racing to the living area where we all bowed our heads to pray together.

We had a wonderful time together during the holidays; I cherished the Ngqungwana family reunions and the memories we shared.

After all the festivities of December, the new year came, bringing with it a new chapter in my life: I started at Isaac Booi Senior Primary School during the third week of January. I wore black trousers with a white shirt, a long maroon-and-gold-striped tie, and a matching maroon jersey with gold, green and white stripes on the neckline, accompanied by the requisite school badge that read 'Determination Breeds Victory'.

On the first day of school, which started at 7 a.m., we followed the teachers to assembly, where one teacher led us in singing hymns from our pocket hymnals. Afterwards, the teacher introduced us to the principal – a tall, dark-skinned, stern-looking man, and a brash and succinct speaker, almost like a drill sergeant ready for a culprit on whom to test his will and authority.

'Education is very important, and if you are a pupil in this school, you must be proud of that. I love children who behave, but I will not tolerate disobedience. Do you hear me, my children?' he asked.

'Yes, Principal,' we replied meekly, nodding our heads in unison.

Women had instructed us at my primary school, and I realised that this new school had quite a macho hierarchy.

Later that day, the music teacher at the school, who carried himself regally, stopped in at our classroom and asked us to sing the hymns from the morning's assembly in a group.

I backed away so he couldn't see me, and mumbled to myself, shaking my head: 'What's the use? I hate this school already.'

As we were singing, he made his rounds, coming up close to listen to us as individuals. He lingered near me as I sang, reading from my hymn book. He then patted my shoulder and whispered, 'See you at choir practice after school today!'

It only dawned on me much later in the day that it had been an audition.

When the school day concluded, I ignored the music teacher's invitation, choosing to walk home instead, only to receive a summons for detention the following day after school for playing truant. I was interested only in rugby, not in the music teacher's request. I was not particularly good at rugby. I wasn't athletic enough – well, not athletic at all. Fooling around with friends on the streets was not the same as dealing with a structured game, but I'd happily have tried out for rugby at school, even though I wouldn't have made the team.

I won the battle for opposing choir membership when the school required us to rehearse during the autumn holidays. I knew I had to devise a compelling excuse to get out of the audition. However, fate was on my side. Phumlani, who had been released from Robben Island Maximum Prison in 1991, was getting married in Hammanskraal, a rural town about 45 kilometres north of Pretoria. Christina, his fiancée, was of the Batswana tribe, found in the northern parts of South Africa and in Botswana.

The wedding was a valid and formidable weapon to use. It was

PRIMARY SCHOOL

a real event – it was not happening at that exact time, but no one would be any the wiser. I deployed my strongest weapon, my grandmother, to write a letter addressed to the teacher. I dictated the terms, as she was not the lying type and was uncomfortable with the plan. I needed only her handwriting and signature.

There was great reverence for members of the ANC and MK, its military wing, in the townships, and Phumlani was one of these. They had fought for our freedom and many had paid with their lives. No music teacher would dare deny such a request, I thought.

I ended up not needing the letter. Either the teacher paid no attention, or maybe I was just not worth the trouble because I wasn't that talented. Who knows? I had what I wanted, though: I was out of the choir.

For the rest of the year, I focused on my studies. I enjoyed working with my physical-science and maths teachers. We learnt how to solve equations, and I was introduced for the first time to geometry and trigonometry, and Isaac Newton and Albert Einstein, the laws of gravity and the theory of relativity, and more.

On Thursdays, the boys would all go to Iqhayiya Technical College, along with boys from other middle schools, to learn trades such as motor body repairing, electrical engineering, woodwork, plumbing and carpentry; the girls stayed at school to work on knitting and study home economics.

Though I realised my love was for maths, physical science, geography and history classes, I found Xhosa poetry, and narratives, fascinating. Fortunately, we had very innovative teachers. The ANC had won the country's first democratic election just the previous year and, now that more opportunities would present themselves, our teachers encouraged us to open our minds and become whatever we desired to be in life.

# Chapter 4

# Dancing with the choir

During Grade 6, a new music teacher joined us when our former teacher took up another post elsewhere. The new teacher, Ms Thunyiwe January, may have had a role to play in softening my stance of not wanting to be in the choir. She was pretty: a strong, dark woman. I saw a semblance of my grandmother in her spirit; I liked her immediately. A girl I liked, Sesethu, was also a member of the choir. This sealed my fate. I had few opportunities to connect with Sesethu – joining the choir seemed to be the most workable and logical choice.

In a short break during rehearsal, I worked up the courage to talk to her. I closed my eyes to summon the last vestiges of my courage and, as soon as I opened them, I walked up to her.

'Hey, Sesethu, baby, come join me outside. I want to talk to you.'

From her glaring eyes, I knew I had failed her test. Yet she was gracious enough to follow me out of the choir room to the porch outside, where she listened patiently to my speech: 'Here's the thing, sweetheart, I'm head over heels about you. I've been looking at you since last year, but you were always too busy to approach. I am happy to have this chance now. The two of us are compatible! Let's get it on.'

It was a miracle she didn't slap me outright. What she did, instead, was put me in my place.

'Listen, Ngqungwana. Do not act as if you know me. First, you are vulgar, and second, that is no manner to address girls. You're not even my type! Leave me alone.'

Things were not going as I had planned, but I was too stupid to realise I needed to apologise. When my friends asked me how it went, my response was, 'To hell with that aloof chick. She thinks she is so important. I don't care about her. She's not even that beautiful.'

I shifted the blame and missed the lesson; my machismo and ignorance had lost me the opportunity to date her. Whatever she may have thought of me before that moment would have altered that day.

It's a good thing I joined the choir. I learnt a lot from being surrounded by the choirmaster and the women in the choir, including proper etiquette. I befriended them, gaining their trust and confidence before anything else. But I never forgot my faux pas with Sesethu; deep down, I knew I needed to make amends. Memories of the saga with Nomaphelo returned and, while I hadn't been violent with Sesethu, I still knew I had much to learn.

I continued with the choir, even though my primary aim in joining had failed. I surprised myself by soon becoming immersed in the music. Since none of us could read or write music, and had had no formal music classes, we learnt music by using tonic sol-fa. The more involved I became with choral music, the more my life transformed. I made new friends in the choral community and moved away from Bhiza and the circle of friends I'd grown up with.

Through Chumani, our gifted tenor soloist, I met Gcagca, the cousin of Mabuti, one of my former compatriots who lived across from my house. All three belonged to the Old Apostolic Church and loved choral music. I liked Chumani because he was a jolly fellow and had many lady friends. I seized on this opportunity to meet potential dates. Chumani told me about his friend Gcagca from his church, whom he said I'd like because he loved girls as much as I did. I liked Gcagca immediately and ended up joining the choir at the Old Apostolic Church, where his grandfather was a church elder.

My grandmother was not particularly blissful about my decision to join another denomination, particularly the Old Apostolic Church. Though she no longer went to church, she was still possessive about where members of her household worshipped, and this church rubbed her up the wrong way.

'My son, I detest that church and the way they handle their business. Therefore, no one from this house will go join that madness.'

She never gave me any valid reasons for her opposition. But she had taught me well, and now it was my turn to exercise my judgement.

'If it doesn't make sense, and you are not convinced in your heart to follow through, then trust your heart,' she said, resigning herself to my decision.

And so we went, back and forth, fighting about it – but, in the end, she had to trust my judgement. I had always assumed that I was as stubborn as she was, but it turned out that my obstinacy exceeded hers. I joined the church choir, but never became invested in church affairs. I could not have cared less what separated one church from another or which church thought it held exclusive rights to Jesus and to fly in the skies with angelic beings. We were just teen pariahs interested in music, mischief and not being constrained by religion's yoke. Later, I came to understand part of my grandmother's views about that church: it repressed women's voices, viewing them as subordinate to the patriarchy. Even if I had known this at the time, I could not have comprehended gender and class constructs.

My life changed again when I met two other choir members,

Sabelo and Nonkie, who were also gifted. Together, we formed a male a cappella group – Nonkie, Gcagca, Sabelo, Jomo (who was also from our church), two other friends, and me. We named it 'Ultimate'. If you think our choice of name was bizarre, or even pretentious, another male group originating from the church was called 'Ecstasy'. (I guarantee you, they did not understand what that meant at the time.)

We were all so naive then, living each carefree day by what it presented. We were inspired by Take 6 and the success of Boyz II Men; we could sing, and we decided, by God, that we would be the first famous South African R&B group – or, at least, the local stars of Zwide township.

By chance, the student body selected me to be their Class of 1997 representative. I had neither envisioned nor sought this. One day, the principal called me to his office. He told me that, at the next day's assembly, once we had finished our prayers, he would instruct the senior class to stay behind for a few minutes to choose a spokesperson for the Farewell to Middle School ball. I was to count the votes. First, I had to go to all the classes to announce the vote, so that each person had a day to think about it.

D-Day came. The assembly dispersed, leaving all but the senior class. I went up to the podium to count the votes.

'So, folks, let us continue and be done with it,' I announced. 'I'll go through the front row first. Say the name of the spokesperson you'd prefer, and I'll move on to the next person. Whoever gets the most votes will represent us at the ball.'

Busisiwe, one of my classmates, interjected: 'Ngqungwana, why should we go through this process when you are already acting the part?'

'What part?' I countered.

'Folks, do you see what I'm talking about?' she said. The crowd answered with a resounding 'Yes'.

'Then, Ngqungwana, you are our chosen spokesperson. It is settled,' she declared. If anyone else aspired to speak for us, Busisiwe had forever silenced him or her. Her strong personality had sealed the deal.

I downplayed this welcome victory, but jumped for joy inside.

I foresaw an opportunity to shine in my social circle and win Sesethu over when a decision had to be made regarding the entertainment options for the ball. I could see some stumbling blocks in my way, however. Two of our group's members were already in high school, and neither Gcagca nor some of the other members of our group attended Isaac Booi. It would not be protocol for us to perform at the ball; I expected the principal to be averse to the idea, just to be difficult. However, the urge to impress Sesethu overwhelmed me.

I had an idea: I would approach Ms January, and we would enchant her with our own arrangement of the hymn 'At the Cross', which we would perform in our home language. I asked the boys to come to my school just after choir practice to surprise her.

The day came. I had already arranged with the caretaker to let my friends onto the premises – my newfound leadership had come with some advantages. Ms January was having a late lunch in the choir room with another teacher, one of her friends. As we entered, she looked up and gave us a stern look – the kind that said, 'How dare you, young boys?'

'I beg your pardon, Ms January. Please forgive us for the intrusion. We want to sing something for you, and we ask for just three minutes of your time,' I said. Before she could answer, Nonkie, ever the impatient one, started the song; the harmony followed. The music overtook Ms January just as she wanted to cut us off.

Once we had finished, she gave her comment: 'That was beautiful, but if you ever disrespect me like that again, I'll have your heads on a platter. Do you hear me, boys?'

'Yes, Miss,' we replied.

'So, tell me – what are you up to?' she continued. 'Are you up to your tricks again, young man?' she said, looking straight at me.

'No, Miss. Just needing your help to convince the principal to let us sing at the farewell function, at no cost. We want to showcase our group.'

'If you behave, I can do that for you.'

We thanked her and left her to finish her lunch. She was true to her word: she helped us impress and persuade the principal.

On the day of the ball, I went over to Sabelo's house at 1 p.m., several hours early. Besides being a singer, Sabelo was also a great barber. I still had hair, and I preferred the German-cut hairstyle; when Sabelo was done, I looked like a young punk, ready to cause mayhem. The other boys also converged on his house. We dressed to impress in our black suits, white shirts, matching red ties and shiny, black shoes.

At his house, we had a thirty-minute warm-up rehearsal, followed by a great send-off lunch prepared by his grandmother. I loved her so much; she reminded me of my own grandmother. It's fair to say I had a soft spot for all the strong black women who raised us with such care. At about 4:30 p.m., we headed for the school to test the stage, do a soundcheck and plan our positions. I also had to recite my speech for my fellas before performing it at the function later.

It so happened that, as we were rehearsing, Sesethu came into the vicinity. When we left the hall, she was outside with a friend. I greeted her and asked if I could have a minute with her; she obliged.

My friends were gracious enough to give us space while keeping her friend company. I thought it would be a perfect time to apologise to her, and so I did. But no amount of poetry, singing or repentance from the new Chief would convince her to go on a date with me.

'I forgive you for how you treated me last year, and I have nothing against you. I am happy about your musical talent and I wish you a successful future. But, I still maintain that I want nothing to do with you. You are still not my type. Goodbye.'

Her response crushed what little pride I had; she took her friend by the hand and left me standing there. Before I turned around, I conjured up my courage so that my friends wouldn't see my defeated look. When they asked me how it went, I told an outright lie.

'She's now my girlfriend!'

They whistled and congratulated me. They were in high spirits and ready for the ball.

After all the formalities and the dignitaries' speeches, it was time for our performance.

The audience had never heard our sound – our mix of indigenous Xhosa music and R&B. Sabelo was our lead singer. I sang baritone, which, in our style, was not too low for my otherwise tenor voice. Jomo was our bass. We left him to play with the low notes while the other boys filled in the rest with their beautiful harmony and counterpoint.

My speech before our performance had impressed the school board. I had fashioned it from the inspiration I drew from Xhosa poetry and the work of notable poets like S.E.K. Mqhayi – a patriot concerned with African renaissance and unity, who was also a historian and considered the Shakespeare of Xhosa poetry – and J.J.R. Jolobe, who blended Xhosa nostalgia with the present and experimented with form in a way that made him an innovator in his own right.

After the farewell ball, because of the fame we had generated in that small pond, we were motivated. For the next two years, I had to maintain the lie about Sesethu, though I suspect my friends knew all along. They just never brought it up.

---

The televised talent search called *Shell Road to Fame* had launched the careers of some prominent South African artists. We decided to enter the contest when we heard it announced on the radio. In our area, it was to be held at the Feather Market Centre, a historic venue in which the Eastern Cape Philharmonic Orchestra performed its concerts. We were serious about our prospects and envisioned using the contest to get our name out there so that people would recognise our talent.

On our arrival, we noticed a ton of people in attendance. Many gospel groups had brought instruments and choirs of sixty or more.

In the waiting room, we probed, with our side-eyes, what the other groups were doing, but we never spoke to anyone. When the stage manager called us, our walk to the stage was a jovial, overconfident one, flanked by young punks from Zwide and Kwazakhele townships.

We had chosen a ten-minute song, which started off slowly and, by the end, would show off everyone's abilities. Sabelo started the song. We all hummed along, ready to sing the refrain that would showcase our harmonies.

Then: 'Thank you. Next!'

To our horror, disappointment, embarrassment and anger, they had cut us off after twenty seconds. We did not know about the time limit for songs, and that the judges could cut you off in the middle of your song if they had heard enough. It was not their problem whether you were ready to stop or not.

Our exit was a walk of shame. We tried to hide our faces as we passed beautiful girls and other performers who were still waiting their turn. None of us got the phone numbers from girls or the callbacks from the judges we had hoped for. The gloom that hung over our group as we returned home lasted for the whole week. Then, the finger-pointing started. We fought among ourselves and took a good month to get over it.

But soon, we picked ourselves up and started afresh. It wasn't the end of the world. Next year we would try again – armed, this time, with knowledge about the inner workings of the audition process. However, two weeks later, Jomo quit the group, citing church duties and other vague reasons. It was a huge blow; he was a talented fellow and an asset to the group.

Nonkie suggested a replacement: Andile, a quasi-friend from Kwazakhele township. His voice may not have been raw and big like Jomo's, but he sang well enough to make an impact and had a good sense of musicality. So, he carried the torch; we continued to grow as a group, performing at local gospel and R&B concerts and events.

Andile was passionate about branding and marketing our group. Our vision of becoming Zwide and Kwazakhele's Take 6 was more than just lip service to him – he had ideas, and we liked him for that. So, we approached local radio stations and community leaders, making our presence known and letting them know that we were available to perform at community events whenever they had them. Weddings, parties, church activities, political rallies, singing the national anthem for sporting events, whatever – we made ourselves available.

When we had built a good audience, we planned our first recital, which we would present at Daku Hall, a community venue about three and a half kilometres from my home. We had scheduled a series of rehearsals. One Saturday, at three in the afternoon, Nonkie didn't show up. This was very unusual for him. After waiting for about twenty-five minutes, we went to his house, two blocks away from Sabelo's house. We found his mother crying on the veranda. Shocked, we all ran to find out what had happened. I thought, 'Jesus, let it not be death or a horrible accident.'

'My sons,' Nonkie's mother said, 'I'm sorry to have to tell you this, but your friend was arrested early this morning. The Detective Branch woke us up at 4 a.m. with a warrant for his arrest. It's a misdemeanour charge from last year. Since he has been spending time with you, he has abandoned that life. But then, every action has consequences, so he must pay his penance. I was just surprised that they sent their big dogs to arrest him, instead of regular police – as if he had committed a hefty crime.

'His fingerprints led them here. But don't you worry, my children. I could see how disappointed he was. The last thing he wanted was to disappoint you. Please pray for him and keep him in your thoughts.'

We left his house heavily burdened and decided there and then to postpone the concert until his return, hoping he would still be interested.

As downtrodden as these unwelcome developments made us feel, we were not surprised. Nonkie, like all of us, had grown up in a rough neighbourhood, where getting arrested was not uncommon. We realised we still had many demons to fight. None of us judged him; instead, we honoured his mother's request and prayed for him. When I told my grandmother, she prayed for him every day until his release.

As I sought to understand Nonkie better, I found out that his maternal uncle was tough on him when his mother was at work – she often worked overtime to put food on the table. So, he avoided spending too much time at home. Like me, he had older peers; they'd reeled him in, onto the wrong side of the law, and he'd got into trouble.

The problem with demons is that they come in the night when you are alone. If you are weak-willed, you will always fall victim to the same situations. But I am convinced that this was his last step downwards. He believed the words in Charles Tindley's hymn: 'I'll overcome someday.'

# Chapter 5

# High school

With middle school behind me, I embarked on my first year in high school at Khwezi Lomso Comprehensive School on Uitenhage Road, directly across from Vista University, now a campus of the Nelson Mandela Metropolitan University. Uitenhage Road links Uitenhage – a town where Volkswagen South Africa and Goodyear, the tyre company, have plants – with Port Elizabeth.

My mother's sister, Xolisiwe – who was now working for the Department of Social Development, having finished her studies at Fort Hare University in Alice, two hours from my home town – had come to live with us. My mother and her sister had always had a precarious relationship. One day, they were best friends; the next day, they hated each other. Whenever they fought about something small, an ugly scene ensued, which would escalate as they remembered past deeds.

Now, both have theatrical voices, so they projected when they argued and would go at it for what would seem like an eternity. When you investigated what had caused the fight in the first place, you found it was an inconsequential and minuscule issue that was easy to resolve. I would see my grandmother trying to intervene, sometimes to no avail, as both sisters acted like deranged beings who wanted the last word. When that happened, I left the scene; I had seen it all before.

ODYSSEY OF AN AFRICAN *Opera* SINGER

I believe that most people in my family have a short fuse. I discovered this in myself and had to work something out so I could remain civilised in the real world. Sometimes, I would react to things without dissecting or understanding them. I was not keen, then, about people telling jokes about me. I was a fat boy and did not appreciate jokes about my weight. Whenever someone said anything I did not appreciate, I would punch him before I figured out it was a joke.

When I started high school – and met new people, potential friends and an abundance of girls – I realised that aggression and machismo would not work. Fortunately, the school had a choir, which I joined. On the first day of choir practice, I discovered that there was no choirmaster – at least, not in the traditional sense. It seemed the teachers either weren't interested in leading the choir or didn't have the expertise to do so. Moreover, the school was pro-sports.

Fortunately for us, though, many members of the school choir were also part of community choirs. An alumnus of our high school, Ntsika Godola, was passionate about community investments and donated his time to help train us; we made our schedule fit into his.

There were rules, however, about who could lead the choir in school choral eisteddfods – this had to be a registered schoolteacher. We were lucky, again, in that a student teacher who had come to do his practicals at our school loved music, so we recruited him as our official choirmaster. Ntsika would train and prepare the choir, and the student teacher would take care of the formalities in the competitions.

I remember rehearsing 'From the censer curling rise' from Handel's *Solomon*. It is a high piece. A tenor then, for the first time I had problems singing its high notes. Unbeknown to me, my voice was changing to baritone. I sensed something was wrong and felt inclined to stop singing for the rest of the year. I had no singing teacher – just a gut feeling that I should not push my voice until I felt better. It is a good thing I followed my instincts, or I may not have been here, writing this book as an opera singer.

I was embarrassed to admit I could no longer sing those notes. A bass in the choir didn't help: 'Musa, chap, what is going on with your voice? What is with the pharyngeal and guttural singing when you approach high notes?' There was raucous laughter from the rest of the boys and a look of pity from the girls. I was hurt, but I saved face and pretended it didn't bother me. But when I got home that evening after rehearsal, I cried in the darkness.

There and then, I quit the choir. I told no one; when they did not look for me in the days that followed and I missed practice, I figured I must either have been terrible, or they didn't care. I stuck with my decision, confused and disappointed.

I was also becoming less interested in the Old Apostolic Church; I was only there for the choir. I often felt cut off by what I had determined to be the priests' obnoxious views of the world. The church constantly preached Matthew 5:13 to us teenagers: 'You are the salt of the earth. But, if the salt loses its saltiness, how can it be made salty again? It is no longer good for anything, except to be thrown out and trampled underfoot.' Apparently, being the salt of the earth was limited to being confined within the church, and our wanting to develop our talents outside of church activities was forbidden for being 'worldly'. The priests often talked condescendingly to us. We could not ask questions or challenge them: it was considered rude to do so.

The church was so authoritarian that I developed a strong distaste for it. I always followed my heart, so I decided one day to part ways with the church. The first thing I did was to tell my friends and fellow church choir members I was leaving, and that the decision was final. They tried to convince me otherwise; some even tried to convince me that I would lose my name and place up yonder with the saints. I forged ahead, without a care in the world about eternal judgment or the rapture.

I have learnt, over the years, to intersperse my stubbornness with grace, patience and a smile, despite having made an executive decision inside to veto any proposals that I feel strongly against. The priest who oversaw my choir and was the head of the youth division visited my home with his deacon, thinking my grandmother would side with them. But she told them, politely, that when my mind was made up, there was nothing anyone could do about it. After three months of harassing me, they gave up.

That year, I took back my power. It was refreshing to glide through school without the burden of extramural activities or religious zeal. I could devote all my attention to figuring out high-school life. All Grade 8 and 9 learners followed a general syllabus. In Grade 10, the school's curriculum was divided into three groups – academic, technical and business. I would choose the academic group when the time came; I wanted to study medicine or engineering.

I continued receiving good marks. The end of the academic year found me in the top five of the Grade 8 class: with a perfect attendance record and excelling in maths, science, typing and English. I continued this trajectory, topping it with a national Science Olympiad in Grade 11, earning a GPA of over 3.8 – just shy of the 4.0 required for a chance to go to Johannesburg and compete in the finals, which would lead to a trip to London. I excelled in English as a subject despite, for the first time, being taught in English and not in my native tongue.

Because our high school was a technical one, it required teachers with backgrounds in engineering. We therefore had many white teachers, who came from Uitenhage and Despatch, neighbouring towns where major corporations had their plants. We still spoke two languages at school – Xhosa and English – but often heard Afrikaans, a third language.

With the need to speak English more frequently, I listened to BBC broadcasts and read English newspaper articles to supplement my learning at school. I was determined to improve my communication skills, and to learn, and somehow forgot about choirs and singing.

But then, at the start of the new school calendar in Grade 9, music whispered to me again. I decided that, if I rejoined the choir, I would need to change voice types. Though I still did not understand the language and technique of the voice, I felt comfortable singing baritone. When I felt comfortable with singing at all again after a vocal rest of over ten months, I went back to the school choir.

When I walked in, the same person who had made fun of me the previous year did so again. 'My dear chap,' he said, 'are you not lost?'

I ignored him, trying to channel the new, patient Musa. They all laughed. I could not tell whom the laughter was directed at, but when the choirmaster tested me – in a sort of audition, making me sing a church hymn – I opened my mouth and sang and nobody dared make fun of my singing ever again.

I had also parted ways with Ultimate. All of us had other commitments and had outgrown it anyway. We stayed friends and continued singing in choirs, often meeting up along the way. Nonkie had been released from jail after a few months, to serve a suspended sentence. He had changed schools and was happier. He wanted to start a new life.

Once again, music would lure me away from the temptation to make bad decisions.

Male choir singing is one thing that touches my spirit. The Tri-message Chorale did just that, with its fusion of American gospel and African indigenous music, a cappella. How they carried themselves! The fact that it was a church group did not stop people from appreciating the music – including the girls in the congregation.

Finally, I would learn from real men how to interact with women.

# Chapter 6

# The Seventh-day Adventist Church

The Tri-message Chorale derives its name from the three angels' messages found in the fourteenth chapter of the book of Revelation. This chapter gives a final warning to the world just before the Christians' long-awaited second coming of Jesus Christ, when humankind must choose between worshipping God or the beast. These messages form part of the core doctrines of the Adventist church. So, the messages in the music of the chorale – although they cover a wide range of subjects – have, as their central theme, the lamb, or Jesus.

The male group comprised regular people, most of them professionals in various fields and family men. Among the single men, I was the youngest – a rookie in the true sense when I joined, as I was still in high school. In that choir, I found the support of men I had needed for so long.

Surrounded by older men who had lived a life driven by faith and goodwill, I knew I would learn many valuable lessons. It is there that I learnt the value of forgiving myself before I could forgive others. These men – who knew the value of temperance and did not drink – left me astonished.

I also realised that, although I rarely thought of my biological father, I still carried an anger I needed to release in a way that would not destroy me or those around me. The anger you carry in your veins is very dangerous; it can consume you. The people I encountered here were neither holy nor without sin, but I could learn, by emulating them, how to own up to my mistakes and faults.

My first impression of the church was that the people there were very knowledgeable. Considering that over half of South Africans do not have adequate education, this took me by surprise. They studied not only the Bible, but many books besides, and could explain pivotal narratives and lead discussions with ease. They read and researched, and encouraged new converts to do so too. I was taken in by enthusiasm and a love for reading. The nerd in me had found an avenue where I could be myself without worrying about who was judging me.

Upon hearing about my latest endeavour and meeting the new people in my life, my grandmother was less disparaging than she had been about my Old Apostolic Church chapter.

Where we differed was on the day of the church's services. Seventh-day Adventists not only believe in the second coming of Jesus, but observe the Jewish Sabbath as stipulated in the book of Exodus. Therefore, sunset on Friday is the start of the Sabbath, which lasts until sunset on Saturday. No work goes on during the Sabbath in those circles.

Black Adventists, however, spend the whole of Saturday at church services and take worship seriously. From the days of the indigenous faith, to the time when the missionaries introduced Christianity, to now, black worshippers have been serious about thanksgiving and praise. They fill the whole day with teaching, music, preaching and Bible study, only taking a break for lunch.

While I took to this practice, my grandmother did not. It was one thing for me to join this movement, but another to expect her to observe it too; on Saturdays, we fought.

'Who do you think I will send to run errands when you are in Sunday worship the whole day?' she asked.

## THE SEVENTH-DAY ADVENTIST CHURCH

'Sabbath service, Skuvethi, not Sunday worship,' I corrected her. She nearly lost her temper.

'Do you think you are a big boy who can teach *me* about religion, now?' she shot back.

'I will not argue with you. The decision is mine to make and the faith is important to me,' I countered.

She shook her head, mumbling in disbelief, knowing I was resolute. Despite all this, however, she let me do what I wanted if it did not cause pain to anyone else.

With hindsight, I realise that my learning the value of reading and thorough research through the church has given me access to the teachings of the world. Travelling has also increased my thirst for knowledge. By spending time in different parts of the world and learning about various cultures, and combining that with my own understanding of the parallels between societies and faiths, I came to see that not everyone shares my belief system, but we can find a way for all of us to coexist. This church differed from my previous experience with religion, which was very rudimentary and promoted a narrow view of the world and a lack of tolerance.

One of my favourite songs with the Tri-message Chorale, one that still stays with me, was an arrangement we sang directly from the church hymnal. The lyrics are powerful and the melody itself is soothing and comforting:

Under His wings I am safely abiding;
Though the night deepens and tempests are wild,
Still, I can trust Him; I know He will keep me;
He has redeemed me, and I am His child.

*Under His wings, under His wings,*
*Who from His love can sever?*

*Under His wings my soul shall abide,*
*Safely abide forever.*

Under His wings – what a refuge in sorrow!
How the heart yearningly turns to His rest!
Often when earth has no balm for my healing,
There I find comfort, and there I am blessed.

(Refrain)

Under His wings – oh, what precious enjoyment!
There will I hide till life's trials are o'er;
Sheltered, protected, no evil can harm me;
Resting in Jesus, I am safe evermore.

(Refrain)
(Lyrics from the *Seventh-day Adventist Hymnal*)

To say I am an outwardly religious person would mislead you, however, as I keep my faith, political beliefs and personal affiliations private – unless someone wants to have a dialogue, free of bigotry and judgement, and wishes to learn more about my views.

Even a few years later, I would still feel this way about the church. I remember dating a girl, Thandisa, who was a member of the same congregation as me. She was a senior in high school, while I was a first-year at PE Tech. I took a bus ride from campus one evening at about 7 p.m. to visit her instead of going directly home. As we were making out in the street close to the bus station, one of the church elders – whose name I shall not dare mention – was going home from work. For some odd reason, he had to walk by our route.

Upon seeing this 'disturbing' and 'sinful' act, he took her by the hand and said, 'Go home. It is late.'

He did not say another word – he just shook his head as he led her away from the danger. I found out he had gone to my girlfriend's home with his wife to visit her mother. As concerned parents, apparently, they could not bear to see a young and innocent girl waste her life like that, risking potential teenage pregnancy or having her heart broken by a 'player' like me. He made many assumptions about me and presumed to know my intentions towards her. Fortunately, the girl's mother knew me, and she knew I had every intention of having a good relationship with her daughter.

What this experience taught me overall was that the church was always watching, but there were people out there who knew my character, regardless.

# Chapter 7

# The Viola Men's Chorus

My friends Nonkie, Sabelo and Gcagca had all joined local choral groups that took part in big South African choral eisteddfods after my exodus from the Old Apostolic Church. While they were still involved in church activities, my rebellion seemingly influenced them to spread their wings and get involved with 'worldly choirs'. The eisteddfods they took part in included the Old Mutual/Telkom National Choir Festival, the South African Post Office Choral Eisteddfod and the South African Tertiary Institutions Choral Association (SATICA) Eisteddfod. I still saw my friends, but not as often as I would have liked; my school activities, and involvement with the Tri-message Chorale and other church activities – including dating women of faith – kept me very busy.

Envious of my comrades when I saw them perform in a choir contest, I decided to join a community choir in addition to the Tri-message Chorale – the Viola Men's Chorus, a local choir focused on Western classical and indigenous music repertoires led by Makhaya Msizi, a Port Elizabeth native who had studied at Loyiso High School, where Nonkie had been a student before going to jail.

A tribute is due to Shakes Sampule, one of its members, and Makhaya, its music director, who recognised my talent and encouraged me to pursue music after Nonkie had introduced me to Shakes.

I was doing well academically. At home, they assumed – and hoped – I would pursue medical studies after school; I had my eye on the University of the Witwatersrand School of Medicine.

I recall needing a recommendation letter from my church elder for an application to medical school in Johannesburg. For entrance to a degree in medicine, not only would I need a great GPA, but I would also need to have completed community outreach, with a letter from a church or community leader.

Unfortunately, music would not cut it as a community outreach category – at least, not for medical school. So, one of my classmates – Jongi Tafnie – and I enquired at the local clinic, opposite our high school, whether we could work or be of help there. After finding out we could, since they were always short-staffed, we worked at the clinic for two months every weekday after school, assisting nurses, transporting patients and delivering medications, especially for tuberculosis patients and the elderly, who could not come to the clinic. My church elder kindly agreed to write my letter. Not only did he write it, but he let me read it before sealing it: '... Musa possesses a high work ethic to be lauded and recognised. He has also displayed a keen interest in learning and research as his academic grades would concur; I thus highly recommend him as a candidate for entry into your venerable school ...'

I may still have been a juvenile who needed to learn the ropes of public decorum, but people were already recognising the man I was becoming and I was receiving the critical support I needed. (Not that I didn't get into trouble from time to time, still, however.)

I had loved singing in the choir as a pastime and never intended to take it any further as a vocation. Nor was I aware that one could make a living out of singing. While I was still with Ultimate, we had aspired to become a leading South African group – but, when those hopes faded, we had to face the reality of our situation. Education was the logical next step.

Shakes was a baritone who sang in the Loyiso High School Choir and was also a member of the Viola Men's Chorus. After talking to him about the choir contests I loved watching, he seized on the opportunity to recruit me. So, after much waffling about the idea, I agreed to accompany him and observe a rehearsal on a Tuesday evening. Their style was noticeably different from most choirs, since they focused on Western classical music and read music from regular staff notation – a novelty to me.

To my astonishment, they had female singers there, working on a specific programme for an opera-focused concert. Even though the lads were averse to a mixed choir, they were tolerant of this short-term venture, and no one minded having the beautiful women to look at.

I could see how each chorister was trying to impress the ladies. Even chaps who rarely sang solos had ideas and wanted to impress their guests.

'Bra Kaiser, please, Maestro, give me a chance to sing a solo,' is all I heard, as the men fought among themselves like children in line for sweets.

When the rehearsal was over, Shakes introduced me to Makhaya. I auditioned for him. I initially thought I would audition in front of him alone, and that everyone would vacate the rehearsal space. But, to my surprise, he started playing the piano and asked me to sing scales in front of everyone. I was peeved inside, more than anything. Usually, auditions make one nervous. But I wasn't: my anger transcended that step. What was this? Entertainment for his choir? Was I a circus clown?

As it turns out, that's how they ran their auditions. Makhaya saw how annoyed I looked and said, 'Don't worry, young chap. Ignore the others. We do things this way so you can get used to singing in front of an audience.'

I said, 'Let's get on with it,' and sang the scales. I could hear the chatter from them when they heard my voice. At first, I thought it was to mock me, but I soon realised it was astonishment. Only then did I register that something special must have come out of my voice. And so, I joined the group.

It is from Makhaya that I had my first voice lesson, though he always referred to Cape Town as the best place to get training in South Africa. Makhaya had received a scholarship to study music at the South African College of Music at the University of Cape Town. He was one of the first black students who was interested in studying opera to be admitted to the college after the first democratic election in our country.

Makhaya had not finished his studies, for various reasons, but he returned to our home town, where he rejoined the Viola Men's Chorus. I sang with the choir for two years, during which Makhaya invited several of us to his house to watch an opera performance – our first time. It was a 1978 Glyndebourne production of *Die Zauberflöte* (KV 620) on VHS, which Makhaya had purchased while a student in Cape Town. In this production, Sir Willard White portrayed the role of Die Sprecher. Seeing this art form for the first time, and witnessing a black man playing a major role, inspired me to sing opera; I never ceased wishing to become an opera singer after that. From then on, I felt an internal dichotomy steeping – the two polarising elements in conflict within me were science and my family versus following this foreign art form.

We took part in a festival hosted by the Eastern Cape Philharmonic Orchestra, alongside many local choirs, including a guest male choir from Norway, which presented a joint concert with the Port Elizabeth Technikon Choir, accompanied by piano, in the neighbouring town of Uitenhage. The concert was at Riebeek College, a multiracial girls' high school with a beautiful auditorium.

Our pianist was Mrs Pauline Olivier from the Oratorio Choir of Port Elizabeth. She had worked with Makhaya many times before he left to study at UCT. Makhaya chose 'O Isis und Osiris', an aria for solo and choir from *Die Zauberflöte*; between our sets, I sang this aria.

It was my first solo performance. Watching the other two choirs perform was daunting, and I felt the butterflies, but I did all right. I remembered my first audition for Makhaya, and it paid off to have had that experience of singing in front of strangers. The audience's faces had similar expressions to those of the choir members on the day of my audition. The smiles from the Norwegians encouraged me, and the chatter from the PE Technikon Choir told me I was on the right track.

When we had finished our performance, we moved to a big reception area that had a banquet extravaganza with many delectable foods I had never seen or heard of before. I was trying appetisers when a Norwegian gentleman from the guest choir approached me to say, 'You have a lovely voice, young man. We hope to see and hear you in the opera houses of Europe one day.'

Then, while I was still mulling that over happily, Mthura Majeke, the music director of the PE Technikon Choir, came over as well to congratulate me and invite me to join his choir. I must admit, even though I had not considered joining another choir, my heart wanted to jump at this opportunity. The PE Technikon Choir was a tertiary institution choir made up mostly of students. It was famous for being a champion in choral eisteddfods and I had a rapport with its style of singing. I think what also attracted me to it was that it travelled a lot and was a choir from a prestigious technical college, which was my second choice after medical school. I didn't join at once, though.

After this concert, we formed a mass choir with the orchestra and our Norwegion guests to perform at the Feather Market Centre in Port Elizabeth.

I sang with Viola until my senior year in high school. Later that year, Makhaya left the Viola Men's Chorus owing to internal politics. Since I was new to the group and had no interest in these developments, it seemed a perfect time for me to go my own way and consider Mr Majeke's invitation.

The success of that night, with the positive feedback from the Norwegian choir and the PE Technikon Choir wanting me to join their ranks, had boosted my confidence in solo singing.

In the face of opposition from home about pursuing a career in singing, I opted to apply to PE Technikon. This technical university is now part of the Nelson Mandela Metropolitan University. I must acknowledge that my academic progress had plummeted that year. I had to go through the ancient tradition of *ulwaluko*, which interrupted my preparation for exams. My high school GPA dropped.

For any Xhosa male, the tradition of *ulwaluko* is crucial. It is when the father steps in and assumes responsibility. For me, this would be the last strike against my father. I already held a grudge against him for his absence from my eighteen-year-old life. Nevertheless, I still hoped he would not sink so low as to embarrass not just himself, but also his family.

However, he neither showed up nor helped in any way.

This meant that my mother had to carry the weight on her shoulders. She did it with grace and took care of all the financial responsibilities. We were also fortunate that my uncle, Mncedisi

Ngqungwana, had returned from his studies at Fort Hare University in Alice. Other family members – especially my uncle Eric Ngqungwana, who played an important role for me in the mountains during *ulwaluko*– came to my mother's aid too.

While the *ulwaluko* ritual is a male-only practice, it is customary for the woman of the township, and also for men from the neighbourhood, to join in a vigil of dancing and singing untill dawn, when the male elders and initiates leave for the mountains. And so it was with me as well.

There, isolated from people, my fellow initiates and I lived in special huts for over a month. We were given cloths and blankets for warmth. The elders expected us to observe numerous bans and to obey their instructions. The different stages in the initiation process were marked by the sacrifice of a goat or a sheep.

During the next several weeks, I got used to my new setting, and my uncle checked daily on my well-being, more than filling the void left by my father. Because *ulwaluko* is a sacred, ancient, gender-specific rite, it remains a taboo subject to discuss openly. But what isn't secretive about it is that all its teachings, daily instructions, discussions and rituals centre on the role of men in society and how they can better themselves. These discussions include topics such as tradition, history, ceremonial law, social living and communal responsibility. Thus, up in the mountains, men – even the elderly, who visited us from the townships – behaved differently. They had an authoritative presence and taught us how to earn their respect.

When I returned from the mountains, I knew that everyone would likewise look at me with this same type of respect and reverence; while there, I learnt – accordingly – how to behave in a dignified manner, especially regarding how I would go on to treat women and the elderly. It would take me a while to fully understand these new responsibilities and expectations, but, underneath it all, I could appreciate their value and how they would make me a better person.

The ceremony after this rite is called *umphumo*, which means 'the coming out' or 'the return of the initiates from the mountains'. It is a traditional party; at home, they slaughtered sheep. Women made the traditional beer, *umqombothi*; my grandmother was the lead brewer, and her daughter, my aunt Xolisiwe, was responsible for the cooking. To this day, I can't tell you for how many hours both my mother and my grandmother had to labour as domestic workers to raise the money to buy everything for the ceremony.

The *umphumo* was the pride of my family; the ceremony consisted of traditional songs of joy, and both men and woman wore traditional clothing. The aprons on the women's dresses displayed various colours. They were also adorned with bracelets and beads and, on their heads, wore an *iqhiya*, a cloth that is decorated with beautiful beads. Their skirts were a frothy blanket around their waists, and they wore beaded ankle bracelets and carried traditional handbags. Some men had on a black-and-white blanket adorned with beads. Around their necks, they wore bead necklaces of different lengths and colours, as well as beads around their wrists and ankles.

Everyone in the neighbourhood was invited to share in the food and celebrations. When we returned home in the early hours of the morning with our entourage of male guardians, the men sang songs. Another entourage of women was waiting for us and greeted us with their own gender-specific songs. When the women and men were united, they sang songs that are for everyone. There were children amid the celebrations, and dogs singing in their own fashion.

On my return, I went to my shanty, ready for the ceremony of *ukuyala*, which the older women of the neighbourhood conducted.

There I was instructed on how I was expected to treat my mother and women in general. This can last for over an hour, depending on how many women come to instruct you.

After that, I went to another *ukuyala* section outside, in a place called *ebuhlanti*, a conclave where the men and male family elders gather to take their turn to give instructions. It is also the place where they slaughter lambs and dedicate their blood to the ancestors. They hang the horns in a shaft at the centre of the conclave as a reminder of the ceremony and its dedication to the ancestors. The men, too, gave directives on how to treat women: with care and respect. I also had to have self-respect, and protect the needy and poor. Their last directive was that I should always strive to lead honourably and perform charitable duties and actions, should the need arise.

I also received gifts and some money from a few family members.

People got drunk on the traditional beer, which compares in strength to alcoholic spirits. My grandmother was a master brewer; people from our village called her *umsili*. Her friends often said to her, '*Hayi uyakwazi ukusila nkazana,*' a phrase of endearment meaning that she was good at her job.

The following day, a Sunday, it was the turn of the Adventist Church to come and celebrate with me. The late Mr Tyatya, the father of two of my colleagues in the Tri-message Chorale and an elder in the church, led the service. This celebration with the Adventists differed in context from the traditional one the day before. First, it was alcohol-free, and it was more like a church service.

Black Adventists still celebrate the ritual of *ulwaluko*, but do not slaughter animals to dedicate to the ancestors. Instead, they lead the ritual with prayer. The elder from the church prepared a homily that linked this age-old ritual with the Jewish ritual of circumcision first celebrated by Abraham, his covenant with God and human spirituality, and my role as a man in society, aligning my life with the gospel of Jesus and the covenant between man and God, abstaining from alcohol and living a life of temperance. While the celebration was about me, it was also a platform for the elder to spread his message to the unconverted. A very interesting day it was.

Overall, the festivities were a success, but they were short-lived for me, as I had to return to my school responsibilities. I had lost time at school, where winter holiday classes for the seniors had gone on without me during my time in the mountains. My biology teacher was adamant that I should delay the ritual until I had finished my studies, but her wishes fell on deaf ears; I wanted to get it over with and, at the time, I didn't care about losing time at school. I missed six weeks of classes – four weeks of winter school and two weeks of the regular calendar.

I had to catch up, with limited time; the classes were already finishing up their last modules. I was also stressed about university fees and feelings of anger towards my father. With hindsight, I should have been more concerned with the job at hand. I soon learnt that the teachers had covered a lot of valuable work during winter school, especially in maths and biology.

When I wrote my mock matriculation exams, I scored low marks and realised how little I knew. My maths teacher advised me to change from higher grade to standard grade for the final exams. This crushed my spirit, but I knew I needed to do this to increase my chances of graduating. I was angry and couldn't retain anything new I studied. Reluctant as I was, I followed her advice. I got through my exams and graduated, but with a lower GPA. I passed those exams with pure luck.

And I lost my chance to go to medical school.

I tried to hide my disappointment, but it broke me inside. I became even angrier about my father's absence during this critical time in my life. To this day, he has not apologised; on the few occasions I have seen him, he has never shown any interest in my well-being or my dreams. Our conversations are one-sided, all about him. I decided I could learn nothing from him, and that we had nothing to talk about.

I now have no expectations of him.

I needed to take a gap year: find the space to breathe and figure out the next course of action. I thought it would be nice to earn money while I worked on improving my grades at a community college. Perhaps I could then revisit applying for medical school. At home, however, they saw taking a gap year as a step backwards. My family feared I would become one of a staggering number of drop-outs and never go to community college.

They had also stigmatised community colleges. Their unbelievable attitude forms part of our history: we had been indoctrinated to hate ourselves and emulate things and people we couldn't be. To them, community college was an embarrassment, but it was something I needed. Underlying my need for a gap year was also the fact that we could not afford tertiary education and did not have access to enough credit for a loan.

However, my mother was committed to seeing this through. I could understand her viewpoint and objectives, but the numbers did not add up. Emotional decisions in this context would backfire. 'My child will not be the laughing stock of this community!' she would shout, without answering the question of where the money would come from, or acknowledging the fact that I didn't have the grades I needed for medical school or a scholarship so that I could satisfy their ambitions. They wanted to talk about their son, a medical student at Wits: 'My son is so smart, he'll be the first doctor in the family.' Because, in fact, my decision to take a gap year killed their ambitions.

I understood that, to them, 'gap year' meant 'giving up'. I gave in, and I applied to the PE Technikon; being a technical college, it had bridging programmes for which I would not require a 4.0 GPA. So, I enrolled in their Civil Engineering and Built Environment department for a year-long bridging course, followed by a three-year diploma and a year of postgraduate studies.

If I was going to be studying at PE Technikon, I thought I might as well take Mthura Majeke up on his offer and join its choir. It turned out I didn't need to wait until the following year, when classes started: the choir was preparing for a choral eisteddfod and had a camp in December. My mother was driving me crazy with her daily complaints; I needed to go away until the start of the new academic year. The camp was perfect. I spent a few weeks in the technikon dormitory with the choir, then went to Johannesburg to take part in the Old Mutual National Choir Festival.

I'd had enough of the emotional backlog my father had caused. That camp helped to cool my head.

You may think that I am being harsh about my father, but I have learnt to forgive myself first, and then to forgive him. This way, I could move on with my life. You can only try for so long, or hope for something – or someone – to come full circle. Then, you must move on.

Whenever my mother has raized the subject of my father, I've had to rebuke her by telling her I want nothing to do with him. Some chapters need closing for others to start afresh. Little does she realise that holding onto the past, or even entertaining unpleasant elements of it, will keep you in limbo and leave you wondering why you never get ahead in life.

# Chapter 8

# The PE Technikon Choir

I joined the PE Technikon Choir at just the right time. Its students came from all over the country and beyond, from as far away as Botswana. Many were Xhosa natives from the Eastern Cape. Mthura Majeke, who led the choir, was a local conductor and choirmaster from New Brighton township. He had studied music at the neighbouring University of Port Elizabeth (UPE) School of Music.

Mr Majeke had experience and talent, and he was an insightful choirmaster who understood how to balance choir voices well. We were preparing for the Old Mutual/Telkom National Choir Festival, a competitive festival of choirs funded by respectively the insurance and telecommunications companies. Each province competed in 'standard' and 'large' categories; the winners from each province then met in the finals.

The finals that year were to be held at the Coca-Cola Dome in Johannesburg, and the choirs would be accompanied by the Johannesburg Philharmonic Orchestra. As the provincial winner of the 'standard' category earlier that year, the PE Technikon Choir automatically qualified for the finals.

Another unique thing about our choir was that, because it comprised students from both PE Tech and UPE, its membership changed every year owing to students graduating, finding employment and relocating to other cities. It may have been cause for celebration, but it also meant that Mr Majeke had to recruit new members each year after graduation – a trying thing to do, as students in a technical institution aren't always that interested in joining a choir.

That year, he needed more low voices and a few sopranos, forcing him to search beyond the technikon's perimeters. There was high status attached to singing with this choir and, though not yet a student myself because the semester hadn't started yet, I conducted myself as if I were.

The technikon's facilities and the auditorium were top-notch. I particularly liked the auditorium and, while it wasn't originally built for choirs per se, it did fit our musical purposes well. Its size was adequate, neither too big nor too small, and it could seat 500 or more. The theatre had an uncarpeted wooden floor so the sound would not be absorbed. We didn't even need microphones for the sound to travel pleasantly. More importantly, there was no echo in this auditorium. You could tell that care had been taken and funds spent to build this place. It differed greatly from my high-school auditorium, where everything was falling apart and one needed speakers and microphones to be heard. When our choir had rehearsed there, the sound was too lively, and the sound reverberations had been wobbly and terrible.

Everything in this large, multiracial institution amazed me. High-school students who had been educated in private and multiracial schools also attended this institution, which I found a little intimidating. In the township setting, we had all pretended it didn't matter where we went to school.

'We couldn't care less about those schools' aloof people!' we'd exclaim, but when we visited private schools, we felt small and were reminded of how poor we were. Seeing the lives of these affluent students, I wished I had come from their backgrounds. However, I had to get over this and focus, instead, on shaping my future.

The choir had separate accommodation at the Student Village, an upgraded housing area for senior and graduate-school students. We had one or two rehearsals a day, as well as physical-training sessions to keep the whole choir in shape, and had the rest of the time to relax. Mthura had a work-hard, play-hard philosophy – when it was time to let loose, he was not rigid, but he was always very strict about practice and treating your voice with respect.

The Old Mutual/Telkom competition had a vernacular category, a Western category and a piece the choir could choose at their own discretion. But the jurors chose the first two pieces. The pieces we prepared for the competition were a Tswana song for the vernacular category, and 'Pronube dive, dei custodi', an excerpt from Luigi Cherubini's *Medea*, for the Western category. The *Medea* piece had a baritone solo at the beginning, accompanied by an orchestra in the finals. The candidates for the solo were Lindile Kula, Luthando Qave and me. Lindile was recovering from a cold during the auditions, and the aria was too high for me; Luthando was the perfect candidate.

After all the preparations, we hired a coach from Williams Bus, a company based in Bethelsdorp, Port Elizabeth, to Johannesburg, which was over 1 000 kilometres away.

Johannesburg is the largest, most populated and busiest city in South Africa. Its population, with the surrounding Tembisa and Soweto townships, is more than four times the population of my home town. The area close to its city hall is at the heart of urban revival; the inner city of Johannesburg remains the largest employment centre in South Africa.

Joburg, as it is known, has trendy, buzzing suburbs with restaurant-lined avenues that cater for fine dining and a refined design aesthetic, and expansive malls – including the acclaimed Sandton City mall – which all combine to make the city a great place to be. Though not much of an outdoor city, being inland and not enjoying the benefits of beaches like those of Port Elizabeth, Durban or Cape Town, Joburg has several parks and nature reserves, Emmarentia Dam and the Walter Sisulu National Botanical Garden among them.

Just north-west of Johannesburg's downtown area, on a gentle hill, lie redeveloped neighbourhoods with exquisite architecture. Unconventional and trendy places like Melville are not far from Auckland Park and are great for evening activities, as well as for lunch. This wonderful village within the city of Johannesburg has a real buzz – restaurants, peculiar boutiques and pavements full of tables are the norm. There was so much activity, cars and people, and a plethora of languages. All eleven official languages could be heard in this city, as well as Shona from Zimbabwe and other foreign languages from the visitors who came from all walks of life across the African continent. It was all rather overwhelming for a township boy from Zwide; I had never experienced anything like it before.

For the first few days, we stayed in a private accommodation close to the FNB Stadium in Soweto, south-west Johannesburg, where it was quiet and secluded and we could work in peace. Then, close to competition time, we checked into a Holiday Inn in the Southgate region of the city, where the sponsors accommodated all the competing choirs, for three days.

The rivalry and tension between the choirs were apparent. I could hear people speaking in hushed voices: 'We are better than they are.' And, 'Oh God, look at those ugly dresses, so hideous,' some of the women uttered.

This was a new experience for me, and it seemed both petty and unnecessary. People were so serious and passionate about all of it.

## THE PE TECHNIKON CHOIR

This competition is to choral societies of South Africa what the Super Bowl is to Americans.

We all had one rehearsal with the orchestra and about fifteen minutes to rehearse each piece; so, some of the conductors, who could neither read nor write orchestral music, had to use their own vocal scores and focus their time directing their individual choirs, while the concertmaster led the orchestra.

The conductor set the tempo and, from then on, there could be no surprises, lest you mess things up with the orchestra. The limited time didn't make everyone happy, as it forced black conductors out of their natural habitat.

There was a lot of muttering from some maestros: 'Alas, the organisers are hitting us below the belt.' At least the vernacular section allowed the conductors to perform their animated choreography.

The standard category – ours – competed first. We did well in both choice pieces, and Luthando outdid himself in his solo, but we came in at second place overall. The East Coast Choristers from KwaZulu-Natal won first place, a decision I suspect is still as controversial today as it was the day it was made. That year, the PE Tech Choir was the best we could have asked for, but winning was not to be.

All the choirs were in the hallways, waiting for the results. When they called our name for second place, it felt like someone was driving spears through our backs. I closed my eyes and felt the heavy sighs around me. But we were not sore losers; we held our heads high, hung up our capes and tried to enjoy the rest of the competition.

I continued singing with the choir well into the first five months of my enrolment at the technikon. But while I had a great time in the choir, I was unhappy at the institution: to my regret, my initial fear about not being able to afford my studies was realised. That year, my little sister Nomatshawe, born in 1996, was starting school.

My mother wanted the best education for her and sent her to an expensive private school. It would not be possible for my mother to pay for my tertiary education as well on her meagre domestic-worker's wages. I took the bus to classes every day, because staying on campus or in an apartment close to the school was out of the question. Then there was the equipment. Anyone who has studied civil engineering or quantity surveying will tell you how expensive the equipment alone is. The laser-level kit on its own costs a fortune.

This meant I would have to borrow equipment from my classmates. How was this going to work? I knew no one in my class. I was the only one in my class from the township; in contrast, some of my classmates' fathers owned civil-engineering or construction companies. It was going to be a very long year. I could not pay my fees all at once, so I negotiated to pay them in instalments.

Things seemed to work out until my fifth month of studying, when I received a warning letter, adding an interest charge for a late payment of the previous month's instalment. To rub salt in the wound, I could no longer afford to pay for bus tickets, forcing me to wake up in the mornings and borrow money from neighbours – most of whom did not have any either. By then my grandmother had retired owing to her failing health, and we could not rely on her modest social-welfare cheque.

Had I communicated my problem to the technikon's student representative council, they may have helped. But since I was neither a member of the student political societies nor interested in politics, my chances were limited. So, I did not go that route. I had had enough; in that fifth month, my family's trust in faith and miracles met my practicality. My mother's ambition and fears were clouding her judgement.

I would finish the year, and that would be it.

My little sister, who had no choice in the matter, deserved an education. I already had a high-school diploma and was resolute on finding my way and making things work, somehow. At home, they didn't support my decision, but it was not theirs to make. Everyone was emotional, fearing that I would become yet another statistic, adding to a long line of dropouts. They were afraid that my dreams would disperse into the wind.

How wrong they were. I decided to follow my heart and tuned out the noise.

Emotions had no place in this necessary sacrifice. My grandmother, though she did not understand my world, knew me better than my mother and how determined I was. I would not be anyone's statistic. I would not let this minor setback and my circumstances affect my dreams and plans. I understood the cycles that needed to be broken and the entrapments that kept me there.

My inner voice erupted and broke the shackles of the poverty mentality. I would follow my dreams with my eyes open; I understood that 'the dreamers of the day are dangerous men, for they may act their dream with open eyes to make it possible'.

# Chapter 9

# Changing gears

There is a high degree of entitlement and expectation enmeshed in the black African way of thinking, which is indoctrinated into the family life of many homes: if one person in a family has a job that his or her family believes pays well, everyone wants to benefit from it. Folks plan their lives around your salary as if it's theirs. If you have meaningful plans for your life and break with this tradition, your family sees you as selfish. We call it the black tax, because people want a share of something they haven't worked for or earned. They also spend money they don't have in the hope that you'll bail them out.

This causes major problems and frustration for those who work.

After dropping out of engineering school, I needed to break free from this mentality. I had always wondered why most people in my family never helped one another when they could have done so. I needed to pause: I was very close to adopting this mentality, and I had to recognise that the world did not revolve around me. I understood the dangers of succumbing to the emotions of the people around me, instead of reasoning on my own. Dreaming about things would not cut it – I had to *do* something. I thought my friend Nonkie, who I knew had also been going through struggles of his own, might get together with me so we could share ideas.

Nonkie had won the National School Choral Eisteddfod's solo

category in Grade 12, now called the South African Schools Choral Eisteddfod (SASCE). After this, the Provincial Department of Arts and Culture awarded him a scholarship to music school. They promised to send money to his personal bank account for bus fare, school supplies and lunches. But the money never came; he was left to fend for himself and ask his neighbours for bus fare, just as I had done.

When Nonkie investigated it, the paper trail had disappeared. How could he prove fraud or maladministration? He quit music school.

Like me, Nonkie had been raised by a single mother. After his parents' divorce, Nonkie, his brother and his mother had gone to live with his mother's brother in their family home. His uncle hated him and was verbally abusive, telling Nonkie he would never amount to anything. Despite being a store owner, he refused to help Nonkie with bus fare and used to complain to people that his nephew was a thief who stole from him.

In a drunken state, Nonkie's uncle insisted that the house belonged to him and that he wanted Nonkie's family out, even though it was a family home with both his and Nonkie's mother's names on the title deed. Had Nonkie's mother's name not been on that title deed, his uncle would have kicked them out of the house.

Nonkie found refuge on the streets; for him, crime seemed to be the only way to create his own life.

However, when he met us in our Ultimate days and joined choral societies, Nonkie found a camaraderie among people who understood him and offered him alternatives. Now, in 2004, he and I were years away from our Ultimate days. Much had happened in our lives, but we had remained friends and were now in similar situations.

Sabelo had dropped out of high school after Grade 11 and was in a similar position. The three of us decided we would do something together, and we became determined to put our full energies into whatever this would be. We loved singing and realised it could be our ticket out of poverty. In that year, the leadership qualities I did not know I had, came to the fore.

Makhaya Msizi, the music director from my Viola Men's Chorus days, had started an opera ensemble in Port Elizabeth, the Glorious Singers. I joined the group first; my two friends followed suit, helping to recruit more artists – which proved to be difficult at first. We pulled in a few, and some of Nonkie's friends from Uitenhage joined us.

Makhaya worked hard to promote the group and secure venues to perform. One place we sang at was St Mary's Anglican Cathedral. There, we met the church's choir director and organist, Eric Spencer, and I was lucky enough to collaborate with him four months later when I made my Handel's *Messiah* debut in his church. After many performances by invitation from different organisations, we Glorious Singers prepared for our own concert, organising it ourselves and dictating its programme.

We were lucky to secure the banquet room at the Port Elizabeth City Hall and free accompaniment from Pauline Olivier. Together, we all helped to sell tickets, handle logistical details and spread the news via word of mouth, as well as with radio and newspaper advertisements.

The night of the performance arrived. It so happened that an orchestra recital at the neighbouring Feather Market Centre was competing with us for an audience. To complicate matters, we had to wait in the backstage room of the Feather Market Centre while an event concluded in our banquet hall. We had only one hour to warm up on site while the staff cleaned and prepared our concert space.

Glimpses of the Feather Market Centre confirmed our fears: the auditorium was full, and our audience was only half the size we had hoped for, but we gave it our best.

From home, my aunt, Xolisiwe, came with my then girlfriend, Bulelwa Lloyd. She was a computer-science major at the University of Port Elizabeth and a fellow Seventh-day Adventist.

While my academic year at PE Technikon was hard and my life was not going terribly well, there was at least one silver lining – I had managed to find a girlfriend. Earlier that year, a church elder had tried to sabotage a relationship I was attempting, so it had come to nothing. But then, it was time for the yearly gathering of the church's regional denominations into a two- or three-week evangelism period, based on the teachings of Jesus and His sermon on the mount, where He instructs His disciples to be a light of the world and allow their houses to illuminate His teachings and doctrines to the world. This translated into my church's belief to recruit new members through revivals.

These camp meetings are a big deal for every Adventist. For us singers, it was always a chance to showcase our ensembles, groups, styles and new songs, and to network with other groups that came from different parts of the country, creating opportunities for us to tour and perform concerts outside of our city and region. Every day of the period had an event, with more events on the weekends, and on the Sabbath, when everyone could attend. The Tri-message Chorale, as one of the most recognised singing groups in the country, always had a spot at these gatherings.

We may have been there for evangelical purposes, but to us young and unmarried members of the group and other young people in the church, it was also an opportunity to mingle and court, if possible. I know many brethren who formed long-term relationships, and even married, having met at these meetings. Being part of the Tri-message Chorale meant people recognised us. I capitalised on this.

This is where I met kind-hearted, shy and intelligent Bulelwa, who had beautiful dimples, a lovely smile and was softly spoken. I was immediately smitten.

Much had changed since I had come back from the mountains. I had settled into this new me. I may be an impulsive person by nature, quick to respond or react, but the process of achieving my manhood taught me the value of patience – and of pondering important issues before I acted on them. Hanging around older and experienced men within the Tri-message Chorale reinforced these values as I received guidance from these more experienced mentors.

My new attributes helped improve my relations with women, which in turn helped me develop a good rapport with Bulelwa, who was introduced to me by a friend. I soon learnt that she was the younger sister of a former Tri-message Chorale member. I knew then that I had to tread carefully – had he found out about us, I'd be in trouble. Big brothers are often protective of their kin and are never into fraternising with people who date their younger sisters. The only people who knew about this relationship were the women in her family and her brother's fiancée.

We had been dating for a few months when the Glorious Singers concert came to fruition. Bulelwa knew me from church, and although she knew that I was part of a well-known singing group there, I hadn't achieved much at that point. I had no job and was a college dropout; trying to impress her, or any woman, by being part of a church singing group had its limits. While Bulelwa was never the type who cared what I did for a living, if this relationship was to grow into anything serious, questions would arise – maybe not from her, but certainly from her family.

Courting in the church usually leads to marriage, and you simply cannot be an unemployed husband. Before you even get there, there are lobola and other bride prices to be considered, and finances for the wedding, and then there is rent or mortgage and life's serious bills to add to the mix. Perhaps I was thinking too far ahead, but she was a computer-science student, destined to finish her education, get a job and make something of herself, while my life, in contrast, was in limbo.

So, while this concert was only the beginning of a new chapter in my life, it was important. It was not going to make us any money, but it was significant in that it was my first attempt at being self-employed and showing my family I had the potential to build something for myself. We had no sponsors, save for the city council letting us use the auditorium. Everything else rested upon us to achieve.

This was also the first time my family and Bulelwa would see me perform on stage and as a solo artist. While I never really get nervous before I go on stage, I found this experience both exciting and frightening. I had to contain myself and practise being a professional, seeing everyone from the stage as an audience member and not as family or friends.

Our concert was a success, despite our earlier disappointments. We all had solos and duets, and sang some ensembles to finish the concert. For my solos, I sang my standard repertoire – well, the only rep I knew at the time: 'Tu sul labbro dei veggenti' from Verdi's *Nabucco* and 'In diesen heil'gen Hallen' from Mozart's *Die Zauberflöte*. It felt great to sing in that intimate space. I realised I relished singing on stage.

We had a wonderful time. The audience, including my guests, left before us, as we had to clean the place up before we left in another minibus taxi.

Unfortunately, the concert resulted in some internal conflict, due to money and mistrust, and these issues divided the group. We did not know how much money our concert had made and, while it wasn't our ultimate goal to make money, we would have appreciated any amount, however small. Nonkie and Sabelo, who did not trust Makhaya as much as the rest of us, had a different vision of what we should do with our profits. They suspected that Makhaya would not be truthful about how much we had made, since his wife had sold the tickets at the door.

Nonkie and Sabelo parted ways with the group, leaving me caught between them and Makhaya. My two comrades accused me of letting my regard and respect for Makhaya cloud my judgement. Makhaya focused on artistry and long-term goals, but Nonkie and Sabelo wanted to divide the money among all the artists immediately. Makhaya, as the de facto group leader, musical director and mentor, meant well, but he was oblivious to the hungriness of our stomachs and how urgently they wanted feeding. Meaningful long-term goals and the reality of the moment were incompatible.

In time, I also needed to venture out on my own. My dream was a ticket out of Port Elizabeth; I parted ways with the group.

From the day I turned sixteen, and got an ID document, I'd had this dream. I remember what sparked it: on the day I went to apply for my ID at the home-affairs department, the queue was very long. Curiously, the queue for passport applications was much shorter. There were about two black folks in the line, five Indian people, three coloured people and over thirty white people. It appeared to move much faster than our queue, which processed matters of identification, birth certificates, marriages and other domestic services. Our queue was full of crying babies and stressed-out people who had forgotten supporting documents or didn't have enough money to pay the required fees.

The passport queue, though, seemed full of travellers, entrepreneurs and proprietors; it appeared these complications did not exist for them. Every one of them, including my black brethren, had everything he or she needed. They all looked important and respected. No government officer screamed at them or patronised them, as they did with the general population in my queue.

Right there, I knew I wanted a passport. Where would I go with a passport? I had no idea. Where would the flight, accommodation, visa and spending money come from? I hadn't the slightest clue – I could not even afford school fees. But I knew I wanted that damn passport so that I could have what those other folks had – a sense of purpose and a vision of a destination.

I enquired of the officer who attended to my ID application about the process of obtaining a passport. He looked condescendingly at me as I spoke, but, by law, he was required to help me, so he gave me the application form and told me about the fees.

I raised the money. It took a while, and many sacrifices, but by the end of the year, I had my passport. It arrived fewer than three weeks after I'd applied; my ID took three months to process.

I told no one at school about this: a classmate once told me I was a dreamer when I said that one day I'd travel the world, and that I'd love to walk the streets of New York City, ride the subway and see shows on Broadway. He shot down my dream with a grim dose of reality, saying, 'Dude, don't kid yourself. None of us will ever leave the city, let alone the province. If any of us are lucky, we'll get hired at Volkswagen, Ford, General Motors, General Tyre or Shatterprufe. Then, perhaps in five years, with your bonus, you can visit Joburg with friends to go see some award show. But New York? Who do you think you are?'

It came from what he thought was a good place, to protect me from setting myself up for a major disappointment. I may have had nothing credible to counter his assertions, but I knew I was right to

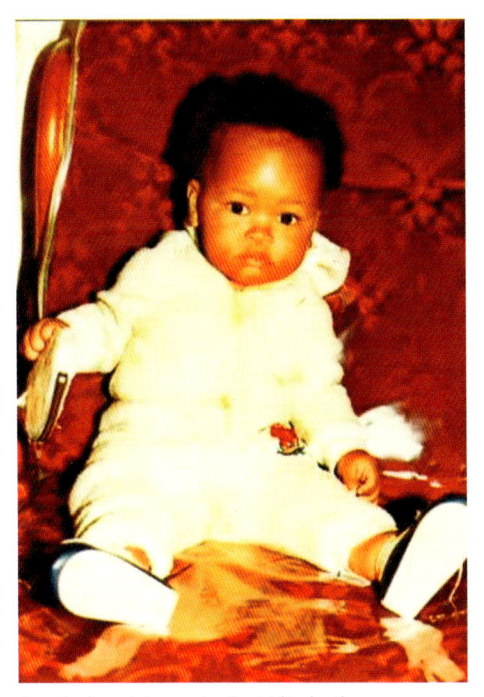

As a baby, at home in Port Elizabeth

In 1991, at Mnqophiso Lower Primary School in PE

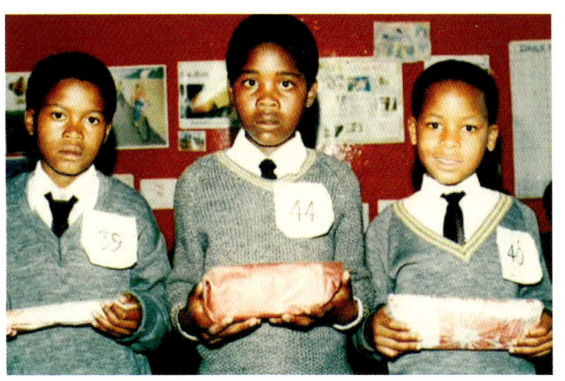

Me on the right, with my schoolmates Phaphama (middle) and Lifa (left), 1994

With my cousin Sandiso in Bhisho in 1993

My first performance with an orchestra: me on the left, with Carmen Erwee next to me, Gill Nock and Eric Spencer at the piano, St Mary's Cathedral, PE, 2004

With members of the ComArt Youth Group at the Guga S'thebe Cultural Centre in Langa Township, Cape Town, 2008

© Shelley-Ann Grammer

From left: Sunnyboy Dladla, me, Maestro Gianfranco De Bosio and Mlamli Lalapantsi at the Teatro Filarmonico in Verona, Italy, February 2009

At my graduation from UCT, on Upper Campus, with Candice Martin, 2009

At the graduation ceremony with, from left, Amanda Osorio, Thando Mpushe, Mandisinde Mbuyazwe and Ncebakazi Dyantyi in December 2009

Me on the right, with Luthando Qave and Chinese soprano Yitian Luan, after the final of the Hans Gabor Belvedere Competition in Vienna, Austria, in June 2010

As Councillor Lindorf in *The Tales of Hoffman*, Academy of Vocal Arts, 2011

With fellow grand prize winner and friend, Sydney Mancasola, at the Metropolitan Opera in 2013

Looking dapper at the Met

Performing at the AVA graduation recital, Philadelphia, 2014

Final bows, AVA graduation recital, with Sydney Mancasola on the left, Chrystal Williams, Chloe Moore, Jessie Nguenang, me and Patrick Guetti, Philadelphia, 2014

At the Academy of Music in Philadelphia with Drs Steven and Ruth Ryave in September 2014

Backstage at the Norwegian National Opera and Ballet in Oslo, Norway, in 2015

With Prof. Virginia Davids and Pretty Yende at the South African College of Music at UCT, February 2015

Backstage with two supers at the Dallas Opera's production of *Moby Dick* in 2016

follow my instinct. So, I had the passport, but it would take me a while to figure out what to do with it.

But reality soon kicked in. I'd finished high school and struggled to raise registration fees for college. When I'd finally got to college, I couldn't afford it. I was down. Distressed, with no plan. Makhaya's group kept me busy for a while. I thought something of substance would come of it. When it didn't, I still had my dreams. That passport, which I had applied for three years earlier, reminded me that I had an appointment with destiny.

The magazines I read, with their pictures of world capitals and interesting facts about them, came alive. I knew New York City was where I wanted to go – I just didn't know how to get there.

Out on my own, I needed something that would turn my dreams into reality. After leaving the Glorious Singers, I found out that Nonkie and Sabelo had not got that far in setting up a new group. They needed a driving force, a responsibility that I assumed. Sibongile Xhathi, a baritone, joined us. An elderly chap, he had also been in Makhaya's group and had also quit. We agreed that once we made money, we would split it among ourselves and put a little into a joint bank account. We also needed a constitution, and funding, and new singers. I created the constitution, which I fashioned off the National Arts Council of South Africa's constitution.

The group from Uitenhage was back.

After much deliberation about a name, we came up with the Nelson Mandela Metropolitan Opera Ensemble. Nonkie and I were to play a fundamental role in setting up our marketing and funding, and in securing concert venues and accompanists for our performances. It sounded like a wonderful plan; this time, we were determined to see it through.

Unfortunately, this took a toll on my relationship with Bulelwa.

She was close to finishing her studies and had brought up important queries about our future, and I was oblivious to it all. Bulelwa was not hot-blooded and forward like me, so she relayed her disappointment to our mutual friend, Mandisa, who did not shy away from chastising me for not paying enough attention to Bulelwa. Survival, opera and my passport dream had become my priorities. I was an imprudent young man not to have noticed the growing distance between us.

I think I expected Bulelwa to voice her frustrations, but she was the quiet type, one who waited for others to read between the lines, and I was not smart enough to gauge these nuances. In my quest to impress her and prove a point to myself and my family through achieving my dreams, I had neglected the most important aspects of a relationship: communication, time and compassion. It was too late when I registered how inattentive I had been to her. I lost out on a good woman.

I remember seeing her in passing several months later. She had finally moved on after Mandisa had told me constantly how much of an idiot I had been. She was with her new man. I knew him; he was college-educated, smart, athletic and had a vision. While part of me was torn up by seeing how happy she was with someone else, another part of me felt happy for her. At least her future wouldn't be delayed by a dreamer like me. Bulelwa saw me too, but what had I expected her to do? She carried on going about her business.

This was a foretaste of my life as an opera singer: relationships would always be challenging, and I would always be caught between chasing my dreams and being with women who had dreams of getting married, starting families, settling down. I took it all in and accepted my fate, silently praying that that man would treat her better than I had.

And then, I continued on my way.

# Chapter 10

# A lucky break

After founding our opera ensemble, I spent less time at home. Nonkie and I knew we needed to get a marketing plan up and running to prevent what had happened to the Glorious Singers at our City Hall concert from happening again. One afternoon, while walking to New Brighton township to recruit members, we picked up a copy of the free weekly community newspaper, the *Algoa Sun*, and came across the name of Monica Oosthuizen of the Port Elizabeth Opera Club.

Monica lived in a retirement village with a full staff of nurses and aides. She was over eighty years old and depended on a wheelchair or a walking stick for mobility. She was a friend of Mimi Coertse's, one of South Africa's foremost opera singers. Monica was an opera aficionado who related to the opera community of South Africa, having hosted many important national opera personalities at concerts and recitals in Port Elizabeth.

Monica had also promoted concerts with members of the Black Tie Ensemble through her articles in newspapers. The Black Tie Ensemble was founded in 1998 to create employment opportunities for young, up-and-coming talent from disadvantaged backgrounds and to preserve opera in South Africa. It was established when the apartheid-funded opera company at Pretoria's State Theatre was closed. The new democratic government had cut state funding for opera companies and orchestras, so Mimi Coertse and the late Neels Hansen, an acclaimed stage director and costume designer, created this ensemble.

We had seen members of the Black Tie Ensemble perform on TV, and many singers coveted a place in the dream team of a new wave of South African opera celebrities. We knew we had to contact Monica to enquire about the organisation and see whether she could grant us an audition – or, at the very least, tell us how we could make our own ensemble in Port Elizabeth a success. While I was thinking of a way to approach her, Nonkie found her telephone number in one of her concert promotions in the newspaper and wanted to call her.

At first, I was apprehensive about us calling her without a plan – I felt it would come across as some form of harassment, since she did not know us. But Nonkie had come up with the idea, and I didn't want to dampen his spirits. So, I agreed; naturally, Nonkie would be the point man for this telephone call. We had some spare change and found a public phone at Njoli Square, a depot en route to New Brighton township.

Njoli was an interesting place to make calls. It was always loud: minibus taxis playing loud disco music and hooting, their drivers using colourful township language and their conductors screaming routes – 'Veeplaas – Soweto!' What a place from which to call a pensioner in a quiet retirement village!

But we forged ahead and made the call. The phone rang, and Monica picked up. Before Nonkie could even explain who we were, with Nonkie's stammering barely audible against the overwhelming background noise, she hung up.

Horror covered our faces.

'Did she really just do that?' we asked ourselves in amazement.

Nonkie faltered when his nerves overtook him. I suggested we go to a different place to try again. We found a deli with a public phone away from the noise and chatter where we could have a decent conversation with Monica.

This time I made the call, apologising for the environment from which we had called her previously and explaining that we were music students who had seen her articles and were interested in the activities of her opera club. Since the art form was new to us, I described our interest in wanting to learn more about it, and I explained that the Black Ties had inspired us. After assurances that we were upstanding citizens and students, she invited us to her home the following day. We were not officially students, of course, but I didn't think a relative truth of this nature could hurt us at this juncture.

In Monica's home, there were enough discs, videos, LPs and books to fill my whole room. These were recordings of world-class singers, from the great Enrico Caruso to Deon van der Walt. Most of us in the group only knew one or two arias, so we had much ground to cover.

Before she could help us, the Diva put us through some intense background checks. Monica was as sharp as ever, despite her age, and had hundreds of questions for us. It was like being in a courtroom answering to serious felony charges. After the question phase, she asked us to sing any opera arias we knew a cappella.

Nonkie sang 'Non più andrai' from *Le Nozze di Figaro*, while I sang 'Tu sul labbro dei veggenti' from *Nabucco*. Taking to our singing, she offered us a concert opportunity in the retirement village's concert lounge. We jumped for joy, for which she scolded us: 'Hey, you kids, stop jumping and making a noise in my living room! Where the hell do you think you are?'

We sat down quietly, holding in our laughter – she was serious. She then made a phone call to someone, speaking in Afrikaans, of which we had a limited understanding. She then told us that we and our crew were to meet her the following Thursday, with one of her pianists.

The following week we went back to Monica's place with our colleagues to meet pianist Kobus Buys from the University of Port Elizabeth School of Music (now the NMMU music school), where Nonkie had been a student. He didn't look like a concert pianist and college professor: he wore farmers' clothes and drove a truck. We soon found out that he owned a farm close to the Addo Elephant National Park, about 40 kilometres north-east of Port Elizabeth.

This time, we met Monica in the beautifully decorated concert lounge next to the dining room, where all the residents came to enjoy their dinner.

The village itself was in St George's Park, close to the cricket stadium – a wealthy neighbourhood. At least five other women – who were friends of Monica's, and residents of the village – came to listen.

'*Here God, maar julle kinders kan regtig sing*! (Good God, you kids can really sing!)' the pianist exclaimed when we had finished singing. That was a relief. '*Maar julle sal nog baie musiek nodig hê om hierdie konsert te laat werk* (But you're going to need a lot more music to make this concert work),' he continued.

With his help, we scrambled for ensemble work and *arie antiche* (old Italian songs) to make up our repertoire.

Our first rehearsals were at Monica's house. To advertise the concert, Monica used the village bulletin and called her friends who worked at the *Algoa Sun* and the *Port Elizabeth Express*.

Monica advised us not to charge the patrons, but rather to use the silver collection: people would put whatever donations they wanted to make in a hat. The plan worked wonders. One of Monica's friends took up the collection after the concert while we mingled with the patrons.

Kobus offered his services for free. He gave us his contact details and let us know he'd be interested in working with us again. Without hesitation, we agreed. Someone of his calibre offering his services for free was incredible. Now, we needed a high school with a piano, and permission to use it. We soon secured a rehearsal space at Kwazakhele High School through the music teacher, whom Nonkie knew.

The period we spent rehearsing, learning and preparing music with Kobus was a fantastic one. We benefited greatly from his expertise and generosity.

When I left for Cape Town a year later, Kobus continued working with our group to produce concerts at his workplace (UPE) and the Hopefield Country House, his business in Addo. In 2013, on a summer vacation to Port Elizabeth, I collaborated on a recital with him and one of his students, a young master's degree soprano named Liske Potgieter. The concert was a stupendous success. In that concert, we also performed an aria from Péter Louis van Dijk's *Windy City Songs*, with the composer and his wife, Junita van Dijk, present. I keep in contact with all of them to this day, and we have a strong relationship.

Through the concert at Monica's village I met Robert Leonard, a retired tenor who had worked in Bloemfontein. Robert had worked in the opera field before the government cut off state funds for opera in 1994 and had been back in our home town for years, working for the government. One of the concerts we did at the Port Elizabeth Opera House through Monica's contacts was with Robert.

I have also kept in contact with Eric Spencer from St Mary's

Anglican Cathedral. Eric needed a bass soloist for this concert and gave me the opportunity to make my Handel's *Messiah* debut in it, teaching me the music and availing himself to help prepare me for the big day. Robert was the tenor soloist, Carmen Erwee the mezzo, and Jill Nock the soprano. I also had the privilege of working with Richard Cock, a celebrated South African conductor. This was a daunting task, as I was not a well-trained singer at this point. My colleagues sang in the ensemble doing the choruses.

Nonkie was always with me at rehearsals. We may have lived in the township, but we were always downtown during the week, looking for funding opportunities for our ensemble. We received many encouraging responses. Some never materialised, but we forged ahead.

Nonkie was astute, street savvy and a fast talker. He used these innate skills to come up with a creative marketing strategy. His cunning still baffles me to this day. He also had his comic elements. These included avoiding certain walking routes and streets in the township, because he owed people money and didn't want to run into them. He would lie about things when caught unawares, saying, 'My revered older brother, this is my friend, Musa, whom I told you about. He will explain the situation to you.'

Nonkie often got me involved in these schemes, even though I didn't want to be. I had to be his alibi and tell his lies: 'We're getting paid today and we'll pay you double when we return tonight.'

He would pay his loans eventually, because I forced him to, but always reluctantly.

To this day, it puzzles me why Nonkie chose store owners, who were also powerful men, for those loans. When they saw us, they were always fuming, as they thought we had robbed them in broad daylight: 'Listen, young Momo, where is my money? Do not double-cross me or there will be consequences,' we were often warned.

## A LUCKY BREAK

Nonkie learnt how to become even more street smart when he landed a temporary job through a very dodgy insurance company selling funeral policies. They had somehow found ways of selling a product and incorporating the five and eight systems, which were methods designed to convince folks on the street why it was important for them to buy the insurance and why their lives depended on it. I learnt these approaches from my hustler best friend, which is how we got people to lend – or donate – us bus fare. I had graduated from apprentice to grand master; soon, I would be the one presenting the pitch to store owners. When we had done gigs, we sometimes returned the money with interest.

The *Messiah* rehearsals with Mr Spencer were taking shape when Richard Cock arrived from Johannesburg. For a white man, he surprised us with the perfect Xhosa click sounds he made when he pronounced *Qhude manikiniki*. This was to calm my nerves, as he could see I was shaking. Mr Cock is a tall man with a commanding presence, but he managed to calm me down. Experiencing that performance of Handel's *Messiah* turned into an unforgettable moment for me and my colleagues. It was my first solo work with an orchestra and a leading conductor. There were music aficionados and critics in the audience, the music was all-encompassing, and I felt great – as if I belonged on stage. The performance further cemented our relationship with Mr Spencer and started a new working relationship with Mr Cock. My life was changing: I felt I was standing on the threshold of some big adjustments.

The reviews of the performance were encouraging, including this one from the official gazette of the Anglican Diocese of Port Elizabeth: 'The four soloists, Jill Nock (soprano), Carmen Erwee (alto), Robert Leonard (tenor) and Musa Ngqungwana (bass), were superb, as was the choir of nearly seventy singers …'

I was to perform with Mr Cock on two more occasions. In 2005, when I was a student in Cape Town, he invited me to sing as a soloist for his annual Last Night of the Proms with the Eastern Cape Philharmonic Orchestra. I sang 'Some Enchanted Evening' from *South Pacific* and 'I Got Plenty o' Nuttin'' from *Porgy and Bess*. The second time was in the summer of 2013, at the same festival, when I was home for the holidays. When I was a student at the Academy of Vocal Arts (AVA), he was very helpful in funding me frequently through the Apollo Music Trust, to which I am indebted for its immense generosity.

Following the *Messiah* concert, we visited Monica, who could not come to the concert owing to her age and restricted mobility. It became a tradition for me and Nonkie to visit her and her friends at least twice a week. They appreciated having these young men visiting them; we would help them with their chores and sing for them.

Monica was to play yet another major role in my life when she put us in touch with Mimi Coertse and the Black Tie Ensemble. At Monica's recommendation, the late Siya Makeke, Nonkie Momo and I were to audition for Mimi and her organisation in Pretoria. We were hungry for it and felt ready to start a new chapter. The Nelson Mandela Metropolitan Opera Ensemble was sturdy, with many teachers who had joined the committee. I felt my work there was done, and here was an opportunity for me to take my singing to the next level. As part of the executive of the ensemble, I was one of three signatories for all bank transactions; I relinquished my signing powers.

Siya, Nonkie and I approached the mayor of Port Elizabeth, His Excellency Mr Nceba Faku, for assistance with what lay ahead. We did not even have an appointment and followed no protocol. Instead, we met him in the parking lot, after he finished work for the day.

## A LUCKY BREAK

Mr Faku was part of the ANC, so we could use some of our family members' credentials to persuade him to talk with us. Ncibane, as we addressed him by his clan name, was a very charitable person, as well as warm and attentive. He listened to what we had to say and asked us to make an appointment with his secretary for the next day. Without hesitation, we followed his instructions; when we arrived the next day, we learnt that he had already made special provisions to accommodate our request – we received return bus tickets to Pretoria and pocket money for our Black Tie Ensemble audition.

Our lives were on the brink of change. It dawned on us that not all our sacrifices had been in vain. There was no guarantee that our auditions would be successful, but it didn't matter. We had the opportunity, and we would sing for our lives. Mr Faku was our saviour, just when we needed one. It was as if he could see the tough paths we had trodden.

# Chapter 11

# Singing for Mimi Coertse

I had arranged to stay with one of my mother's cousins, Xisa Ramafoko, in Sunnyside, Pretoria. She and her husband had offered to accommodate me during my three-day visit. My two friends had their lodgings arranged by their local choir, the Matthews Singers from New Brighton township. There was a choir competition on the same weekend we were to audition for the Black Ties, and their choir director was not pleased that his two star singers would not be travelling with the rest of the entourage. However, the boys assured him that our audition was on Friday morning, which would give them sufficient time to join the choir at the hotel for rehearsals.

We travelled by Intercape Sleepliner, an overnight shuttle bus equipped with comfortable seats that were flexible enough to adjust for sleeping during the sixteen-hour ride. As we left our city that evening and I saw it beautifully lit up, I could not help thinking that, although it looked enticing, I was leaving a life of obscurity for one of fulfilment and recognition. There were no guarantees about the audition, yet part of me felt I was starting anew and that, regardless of the outcome, I would not be returning home from it permanently.

My grandmother had baked treats so that we did not need to spend any money on the road, except on something to drink. Her send-off prayer had given me a blessed assurance. Our days of differences regarding my dropping out of school were well behind us, and the focus was now on meeting new objectives.

As we travelled, each of us reflected on our lives, looking with keen eyes towards our dream. When you have fallen many times, you eventually learn how to balance to find your way. Like a child learning to walk, falling again and again but never giving up, we struggled towards our goals.

We had all had our fair share of strife, I thought as we drove into the night, and had been there for one another along the way, forming a strong bond. There would always be challenges, but we had tools for tackling each of them in a way that was conducive to growth for each of us. Out of all the metaphorical games I had played, I believed, at last, that I had the winning ticket in my hand.

We enjoyed the ride as best we could until we dozed off. I was the last one to do so, being the insomniac I am. We had talked little on the bus ride, but the last thing we said to each other was, 'Sleep well, boys. Tomorrow is a new day. Whatever happens, something will change.' It was as if we had a prophetic gift and were creating new realities for ourselves.

Arriving at Pretoria Station early on Friday morning, we found restrooms where we could freshen up and change into our suits. Our audition didn't start until 10:30 a.m., but we were there and ready by 8:45 a.m.

The security guard in the reception area must have thought we were crazy, as his counsel that we were too early and should come back later fell on deaf ears. Fortunately, at about 9 a.m. the secretary of the Black Ties arrived. He was kind enough to offer us coffee and biscuits, and practice rooms to warm up in.

While warming up, we saw others who had come to audition,

which astonished us – we'd somehow thought we would be the only ones.

'Whoa, gentlemen, are there other people here as well?' exclaimed Nonkie.

'Buddy, what did you expect? That they would give us the royal treatment?' jeered Siya.

I couldn't laugh, as I had thought the same thing as Nonkie. The pressure, now, was mounting; we understood that any singer could win the chance to get into the programme.

Nonkie and I looked at each other. 'Are you thinking what I'm thinking?' he asked.

'Yes,' I responded. '*Shell Road to Fame* at the Feather Market Centre.'

This took Nonkie and me back to how embarrassed we were when the judges cut us off during our act, and how seeing so many other groups had shaken us. But we knew this time was different. Our lives were hanging in the balance – there was nothing to go back to in Port Elizabeth, except hustling and living for scraps. My heart thudded, thinking about how high the stakes were.

They called Siya in first, and then Nonkie. I was the next to last person to sing. On the panel were Mimi Coertse, Neels Hansen, Loveline Madumo (a soprano I had seen on TV several times), and two other people I didn't know. It felt like a special tribunal or a senate hearing of some sort when I sat down in front of them.

It was daunting.

I sang one of the few arias I knew: 'Tu sul labbro dei veggenti' from Verdi's *Nabucco*. I had no comprehension of the plot of the opera or the meaning of the words; I had learnt the aria by listening to a CD from Monica. I imitated what was on the recording. I don't recall how I felt about my singing, but I know that I couldn't look at the adjudicators directly, so focused was I on not messing up my presentation.

When I finished, Mimi called me to sit on a chair facing the panel of judges. It was over, and I felt relieved, but now the jittery anticipation had started. Though I acted like all was well, inside me, doubt and distress were equally at play. Perhaps the panel could sense that I was green and had copied from a CD. My heart continued to pound in my chest.

Noticing how nervous I was, Mimi calmed me by asking, 'Why are you nervous when you've sung so incredibly?'

Incredibly? Me?

Neels Hansen, the artistic director, asked me some questions. 'So, tell us, young man, about yourself. Where are you from? And how do you know Monica Oosthuizen?'

'I'm Musa Ngqungwana from Zwide township in Port Elizabeth,' I said. 'I've been singing in choirs since middle school, before I joined the Viola Men's Chorus, a local male choir in my township. It is where I learnt a little about classical music and solo singing. But I have not had formal music training. My friends and I saw Monica's information in a free newspaper back at home. We contacted her and asked if we could sing for her. To make a long story short, she recommended us to sing for you, sir.'

Though I had been singing in choirs for a considerable number of years by now, I still lacked formal training. Makhaya had offered me some elementary vocal training, but I still did not understand the proper vocal techniques a professional would need. Although Mr Hansen noticed a talent, he felt it would be unfair for the Black Ties to exploit it, as I still needed experience and basic musical training.

Since I did not have college qualifications or training, they wanted to place me in their incubator phase – a programme for people like me, who needed basic training in music. They also put me in the chorus to support principals like Loveline in their productions.

Unlike the principals, the incubators did not immediately have access to individual sponsors who would pay for their accommodation and living expenses. Instead, I would be a 'squatter' at someone's place until I found a sponsor or became a principal in two to three years. Since I knew none of the singers in Pretoria and did not have money to live on, that seemed out of my reach. I was also unwilling to exploit Xisa's hospitality – hosting me for a weekend was one thing, but having me stay with her for a minimum of two years would be unfair.

As Mr Hansen explained all this, my heart sank, and I saw my world crumble before me. Once again, my dreams, which had been almost tangible, seemed to be slipping beyond my reach. But I had misunderstood; they were actually looking out for my best interests and would, eventually, hand me one of the most precious gifts in life – an education.

'However,' continued Mr Hansen, 'recognising your talent, we think there's a place and a teacher who would be perfect for you, and we will supply you with a bursary.' The place he was referring to was the South African College of Music at the University of Cape Town, and the woman was none other than Professor Virginia Davids, the head of vocal studies at the school. She was a well-known spinto soprano and one of the leading voice teachers in the country.

Mr Hansen continued: 'Could you come back on Monday morning? We can then introduce you to these people, and Professor Davids will take care of everything for you. When are you going back home?'

'On Monday afternoon at 2:30 p.m.'

'Good. Could you come and join us in my office at about 11 a.m.?'

I agreed and went to meet my friends outside, discussing what each of our auditions had been like. Realising that mine had gone very differently from theirs, I felt the need to withhold the details and told them, 'I sang and they just said, "Thank you, we will write to you at the appropriate time and let you know our decision."'

Since my two colleagues had had standard auditions, I was not going to hurt their feelings and crush their hopes. We had travelled so far together. I knew that, once I had met with the executives and sorted out the possibility of an education in Cape Town, I would let them know in good time. By then, our emotions and anxieties would have subsided.

My two colleagues were due to meet with their choir and we parted ways after our discussion.

I called Xisa, who came with her husband Humphrey to pick me up. My uncle, Thami Ngqungwana, a chief director at the Department of Trade and Industry in Pretoria, came to visit us after work, before he left for his home in Johannesburg. The weekend was spent relaxing with family and friends.

When Monday rolled around, the Ramafoko clan dropped me off at the State Theatre on their way to work. I met up with the secretary at the reception area, who took me to Mr Hansen's office. Mr Hansen and one other man, who hadn't been at my audition, were waiting there.

Mr Hansen wasted no time and launched into his speech. 'Musa! Thank you for meeting us this morning. We are interested in you joining our company and, if you insist, we will take you, but I must tell you I strongly feel that Cape Town would be of greater service to you. With your permission, I'd like to call Professor Davids at the University of Cape Town and let her know of your audition and interest in operatic studies. Shall I?'

I was momentarily shocked and simply nodded, deciding to resign myself to this unknown territory. What did I have to lose?

Neels and Virginia spoke to each other in Afrikaans for a considerable time. I didn't understand everything they were saying, but I could sense the passion with which Neels spoke when he mentioned my name. I was convinced that I had an ally, fighting for me to have a chance.

After this conversation, Neels gave me a number he'd written down while talking on the phone. I went to his receptionist's office, where they offered me a phone to call Sheila Taylor, the department contact person and the academic administrator at the South African College of Music at UCT. Sheila sorted out my audition times and explained the application process.

I had forgotten that I had actually applied to the university earlier that year, when I was just fooling around. I had written a letter to UCT and asked for their application forms and information about funding and accommodation, to which they had replied by sending me a pack of materials. I had sent off the completed application form and received a letter in return with an applicant number they had assigned to me, but I hadn't taken the final step of setting up an audition. I never thought I'd have the funds to pay for such a prestigious institution.

When Sheila asked if I had an applicant number, I remembered this previous application and found the letter in my file, which I was carrying with me. Sheila then set up an audition time for me. She explained that my high-school matriculation results, combined with my one-year credit at PE Technikon, would be enough to apply to music school.

In the application, I had listed my grandmother as my guardian and supplied her pension information. Since she was over sixty years old, this made me eligible to qualify for a subsidised government loan towards my studies.

After the phone conversation, I went back to Mr Hansen's office to let him know about the developments. On hearing the news, Mr Hansen and his colleague wished me well and made me promise to keep in touch. They both offered to act as character witnesses, should I need them to. I bid them both goodbye and made my way to the bus station.

The ride home was different. I was alone with strangers, since my colleagues had already left for home with their choir. My anxieties had passed and I felt as if a weight had been lifted from my shoulders. I could now look forward to preparing for Cape Town and seeing what the future had in store for me.

The folks in Pretoria seemed to believe in me, and this professor in Cape Town was willing to facilitate things for me as well. It seemed like my prospects were looking up. Now, I needed to focus on fund-raising for the Cape Town trip and finding accommodation. Already, on the bus ride, my brain was spinning as I devised plans in my head. But these would have to wait, as I was exhausted. It had been a long day, and I needed rest.

Back home, and still tired from the trip, I slept the whole day, calling Xisa only later in the day to give her the news that I had returned safely. The following day, I called Monica to let her know about my trip and the outcome of the audition. She invited me to her home, where we discussed plans for my Cape Town trip.

We were fortunate to have had the Mayor help us three boys get to Pretoria, but it would be another thing to ask him for help again. The audition in Cape Town was three and a half weeks after the one in Pretoria, and we all knew that this might not be enough time to organise a concert to raise funds for the trip.

Monica suggested that we call the folks at the *Algoa Sun* to write an article about me and appeal to the public for donations. I was apprehensive about this, much as I was on the first day Nonkie had wanted us to call Monica, as my pride did not allow for my personal business to be made public. Conversely, I needed the funds; I knew pride needed to take a back seat.

I gave Monica my blessing, and she called her friends at the newspaper. Within two days, they had shot my picture and completed the interview, slated to appear in the following week's issue.

In the meantime, while waiting for the article to come out, I needed to find accommodation, and we had no idea how much money would be raised via the newspaper article. I had not been back to Cape Town since the 1991 trip, when I visited Robben Island with my grandmother and Senzeni, so I did not understand where to start with the logistics.

While doing in-service training as a social worker, Xolisiwe, my mother's sister, had worked with a woman who lived in Cape Town. She called her and asked her if she could accommodate me. The woman agreed.

When the article came out, a man called me to let me know he had read it. He asked me how much money I needed. Embarrassed to ask for too much, I asked for just enough for the return ticket, but he still gave me more than that.

And he gave me spending money for incidentals as well. The man was none other than Dr J.P. Hurn – Kobus, as I call him. Kobus had been a concert pianist before he studying pharmacy and medicine at the University of Cape Town. Every year, when I return home for holidays, I meet him for lunch, a tradition we continue to this day; we still send each other birthday messages.

Kobus drew me a map of Cape Town and gave me information about the city. I was now ready for my trip – and whatever life had waiting for me there.

# Chapter 12

# The Mother City

Cape Town – or the Mother City, as it's fondly called – is the second-most populous city in South Africa after Johannesburg. It is also the legislative capital of the country, where the South African Parliament convenes. Cape Town is famous for its landmarks such as Table Mountain and Cape Point, its harbour and Waterfront, its spectacular and natural setting, the Kirstenbosch Botanical Garden, and the Robben Island Museum.

Cape Town also boasts a magnificent arts culture, including the Cape Town International Jazz Festival and the annual Baxter comedy festival. In addition, the city is esteemed for its devotion to classical music, opera and dance, with institutions like the Baxter Theatre, the South African College of Music at the University of Cape Town, the Artscape Theatre Centre, which is home to the Cape Town Opera and the Cape Philharmonic Orchestra, and the Fugard Theatre, named after the acclaimed playwright, one of South Africa's most significant artists.

The city bears a rough history, however, to which the District Six Museum attests.

While riding the Intercape Sleepliner once again, I researched the city, looking forward to being there and indulging in its culture.

## ODYSSEY OF AN AFRICAN *Opera* SINGER

I arrived at the bus terminal downtown at seven in the morning. The bus station is next to the railway station and close to the Grand Parade, the main public square. From it, you can see the Castle of Good Hope and the marketplace with its many vendors, especially women who sell clothes, silk, cotton and food. There is also a bus depot and parking for the Golden Arrow bus company nearby. But, compared to Johannesburg, this place wasn't as overwhelming, and I found it easier to ask for directions. Plus, the black residents of Cape Town speak Xhosa, among other languages, so I felt at home.

There, I sought the restroom, where I put on my suit and tie. I then took a minibus taxi to the university. I waited for about fifteen minutes for the taxi to fill up with another fourteen people. The taxi made a stop in Rondebosch, at the university's lower campus. The University of Cape Town and the Rhodes Estate are on the eastern slopes of Devil's Peak. From there, one can see the southern suburbs of Cape Town, over the Cape Flats and further east towards Somerset West, and the distant Boland mountains. It is a remarkable scene. The South African College of Music and the Baxter Theatre are on the lower campus of the university and are at the cusp of this magnificence.

I spent a good ten minutes taking it all in. It was remarkable and beautiful, and I had never seen anything like it. I considered the residents of Cape Town very fortunate to live under the mountain's magnificent gaze.

Breaking from my reverie, I spotted a campus-protection service station, where I went to ask for directions, finding a man ready to help me. He walked with me to where the music and dance schools were, not far from the Jammie Shuttle, a student bus service that runs between the lower and upper campus. Next to the shuttle stop were two big, identical residences, which I learnt were Leo Marquard and

Tugwell Halls – separate residences for men and women. Opposite them, across from the shuttle stop, was another residence – Baxter Hall for women – and next door to Baxter was Protem, the student wellness service and other administrative buildings.

Arriving at the music college, I discovered many singers outside, some cheerful and others warming up or practising their audition materials. In Pretoria, people were quieter and confined their singing to practice rooms. Here, everyone was showing off.

A few seniors showed me the registration desk and, as I hovered there trying to get my materials in order, a jolly, proper-looking fellow with glasses approached me.

'Musa, I presume?' he asked, with a curiously British accent.

'Yes, sir,' I nodded, trying to maintain decorum. He asked to look at my music before the audition. About five people had sung before me. I heard a great bass voice and, around me, people murmured, 'It's Mandisinde who's singing now.'

Among the group, I looked like a refugee. Everyone else seemed to know one another as they all gathered around the door of the audition room, listening with keen interest.

Mandisinde and at least one other bass before him had sung 'In diesen heil'gen Hallen' from *Die Zauberflöte*, the aria I wanted to sing. But, upon hearing the two of them, I decided there was just too much pressure and competition.

The only person I recognised on the list was Luthando Qave, my friend from the PE Technikon Choir. I had last seen him in Johannesburg, when we competed at the Coca-Cola Dome in 2002, but since his audition time was so much later than mine, we couldn't catch up.

My time to sing arrived. I was very nervous, but I tried to hide it among those strangers while saying little prayers inside. All I wanted to do at that point was get through it without falling apart. I took a deep breath and went in with my bag and jacket. The rest of the candidates looked at me, curious why I did not leave my belongings outside in the hall.

On entering the room – a rehearsal studio for the opera department – I noticed among the panel of judges a very distinctive man with white hair, looking stern and oddly Italian. I gave my music to the pianist, who I later learnt was Colin Howard. He had studied at the Royal College of Music in London and had taught in Britain for years.

I learnt later, too, that the white-haired man was Professor Angelo Gobbato, the director of the opera school and recently retired executive director of the Cape Town Opera. The other panellists were Professor Virginia Davids and Dr Brad Liebl.

Virginia greeted me. I responded with a nod, and she asked me what I would like to sing. 'I will sing "Tu sul labbro dei veggenti" from Verdi's *Nabucco*,' I responded.

I sang with my heart pounding, but by my first entrance I was in the wrong key. Professor Davids immediately stopped me. Having learnt the aria from a recording, I was used to listening to it from the start, with a long introduction. But here, the pianist had given me one measure of music before I was to start singing. I couldn't read music, and this confused me.

I thought this would be the end of my experience. But, realising what the problem was, Professor Davids spoke: 'Colin, could you please start from the top of the introduction?' Mr Howard smiled and nodded in acknowledgement. Then Professor Davids turned to calm me down, seeing how despondent I looked and felt.

'Hey, big boy, you got lost there a little, didn't you? Not to worry, it happens. You're nervous and that's a good sign, because it means you care about this audition. But now, relax and think of us as your audience who wish you to do well.'

I gave myself a silent pep talk: *You have supporters on this panel. Come on, Chief. Do your best. Sing the hell out of this aria and show off your voice. They are professionals; they will know whether you have talent and are something they can work with or not.*

This time, with the long introduction, I knew where to begin. I sang my heart out. On finishing, I thanked the panel for the opportunity and picked up my bag and coat, ready to leave.

I'd just about made it to the door when Professor Davids called out. 'Hey, big boy. Where do you think you're going?'

'Home!' I said.

'No, no, come back and talk to us,' they all chuckled. I must have looked strange, hurrying for the door and carrying a coat in thirty-five-degree weather. There was a chair facing the panel of judges. I sat down and waited for the questions to begin.

In the interview, they asked similar questions to the ones I had answered during my audition in Pretoria. Then Professor Davids asked with whom I wanted to study. I knew no one. Unlike the crowd outside, I was unaware of how anything worked there.

'You!' I said.

I didn't know that people could choose their voice teachers or had preferences based on recommendations. In all honesty, I did not care who taught me if I got in – as long as it was someone knowledgeable.

What I found out later was that getting into her studio was not an easy task and that, in the past, she'd had to turn people away because she did not have enough space for them all.

'So, I've been accepted?' I asked.

'All in good time. You'll hear from us through the mail. We must still hear other students and check whether you've met the academic requirements. But you will hear from us, regardless. Don't worry!' she assured me, having sensed my nervousness.

The panel then dismissed me, but not before I'd asked them a few questions about scholarships and the school itself. I'm sure they must have discussed how bizarre and different I was after I'd left, as I was not familiar with audition decorum.

I retraced my steps to the shuttle station and hopped into another taxi, to downtown Cape Town. There, I boarded a bus to Khayelitsha township, on the outskirts of the city.

It had been a long day. By the time I got to my host's house, it was after 5 p.m. I joined her for a dinner she had prepared and went to bed immediately afterwards. I woke up in the early hours of Saturday morning to prepare for the entrance exams.

In the morning, my host prepared breakfast for me. She must have sensed that I needed time with my own thoughts, as she gave me space to reflect on the day ahead.

Since her home was on the outskirts of the city, I took a bus to the downtown area and a taxi to Rondebosch again. From there, I took the shuttle to the main campus, where I wrote an entrance exam in a huge auditorium. Over 500 students must have gathered there that day to take the exam. I took two of the three allocated hours to complete it.

It must have been about one in the afternoon when I finished writing, and I left immediately for the bus station, even though my bus was not scheduled to leave until 6:30 p.m. I knew no one at the university who would be around, and Luthando had plans. So, at the bus station I got something to eat and waited for over four hours. Exhausted, I fell asleep on the bus, thinking to myself that I would attend to the details and review what had happened later.

A month passed before I heard from the university. By then, I had forgotten about the audition and had given up on checking the mail, thinking that all their talk after the audition was customary and had meant nothing. Oh well, I thought. It is what it is.

Nonkie was more optimistic about the result than I was. On 29 December, a letter delivered by special courier arrived. I had to sign for it. It was one page long, with the words 'College House' written in bold. Nonkie was excited, but I was now more confused than ever.

Then, on 4 January, I received a letter from the Provincial Department of Arts and Culture, where I had applied for a scholarship before leaving for Cape Town. The letter notified me that the application had been approved. The department would pay my registration fee, which at UCT would count as the expected family contribution (EFC).

I would also receive a loan from the government, otherwise known as the National Student Financial Aid Scheme (NSFAS), but that loan would still not pay for everything. UCT's Financial Aid and Scholarship package would cover the rest. Of this, should I perform well, they would convert 60 per cent to a scholarship, and I would be liable to pay only 40 per cent back when I got a job.

The last letter from the university arrived on 12 January. The inconsistency of the timing baffled me, but the letters had come from different departments within the university. I had received residence allocation, notification of the awarding of funds, plus the scholarship from my province, but I still was not convinced they had accepted me. Nonkie opened the letter, as I was being too dramatic to deal with it. When he jumped for joy and hugged me, it was the first time I knew that the answer was yes.

I was so accustomed to letters starting with 'We regret to inform you' that my hopes were not high for this letter. For the first time in my life, I believed I had something special within me. I would be a student at this prestigious institution, the leading African university. I must be a diamond in the rough, I thought, which was why it had taken so long to find me.

I'd had long and dark days. I'd struggled so much. I would not be speaking from the heart if I did not tell you that I despised poverty and wished I had been born into an affluent family. At some point, I had succumbed to believing that I was nothing and would amount to nothing. The fact that neither my mother nor my grandmother had finished high school added further discomfort to this mix.

Getting low matriculation grades and then dropping out of PE Technikon, even though it was unavoidable, had hurt me. It had made me scared of where I might end up. On the outside, I pretended it did not bother me, but most nights it kept me awake – the thought of having no workable way out of the cycle of poverty and failure.

This time, I felt that real and tangible change was coming. I did not know what awaited me in the Mother City, or how I would face it, given our situation at home and my past failures, but I would throw my all into it.

No matter the cost.

# Chapter 13

# Opera School

When I started at the University of Cape Town, Professor Angelo Gobbato was the director of the Opera School. Since I had no formal musical training or education, they placed me in a foundation programme, a one-year bridging course, before I started the four years of study towards a Performer's Diploma in Opera. During my foundation year, I did not deal with Professor Gobbato, as he only taught first-year to graduate students enrolled in the Opera Workshop courses.

Professor Gobbato taught Italian, Diction and Presentation, and Stagecraft classes to those in their first and second years of studying these disciplines. These students also served as chorus members and stagehands for Opera School productions. Our foundation class did not take part in these productions – we needed a lot of academic attention to reach that level. I spent some time with Professor Davids early in my academic career at UCT, seeing her at least once a week for voice lessons.

During my first week at the university, I focused on orientating myself to the entire university and the humanities faculty, which oversaw the music school, and to my residence, College House. All first- and second-tier residences had a warden who lived on site. Since ours was not a huge residence, we did not have an assistant warden. An elected House Committee supported the warden in the day-to-day running of the house, and with the residents' social and academic needs.

This meant that an authoritative male figure would dictate my living terms. I had already been out of high school for over two years, and I was older than most of the residents and the House Committee boys. So, I assumed that having them tell me what to do would be problematic.

I also sensed class conflict in the dormitory system. The focus of the university is on academic excellence and research, social outreach projects and social cohesiveness; but while they were trying to bridge the gap between the poor and the wealthy, working hard at attracting students of all colours, races and classes, there was still a huge divide between students from affluent families and those from poor families.

Programmes and classes are of a high standard at UCT. The administration has worked very hard to put the university on the map, attracting A-rated researchers and scientists, while improving the conditions of the teaching and student bodies. Despite these strides, class conflict is inevitable, as the university is part of a broader society. The student protests in 2015 and 2016, which shook up academic institutions and threatened to close them if no tangible agreements could be reached, unearthed long frustrations from a populace that had been besieged by apartheid policies and then disappointed by democracy's broken promises.

It hurt that the government failed to meet these challenges while squandering billions of rands on questionable projects – that the epidemic of maladministration, nepotism and corruption has seen a few individuals become multimillionaires while students struggle to pay their fees, have no adequate accommodation and still deal with systemic racism. Many have not been able to graduate or continue with their studies because they owed fees.

I was a poor student from Zwide township when I enrolled at UCT, while some of my fellow students and residence mates came from Sandton, Clifton, Camps Bay, Umhlanga Rocks and many other wealthy suburbs of the country. While we received the same education, I still felt the gap – through no fault of their own, however.

I could not afford to go to upscale Cape Town nightclubs. Some of those nights were difficult, studying hard on an empty stomach. Ordering pizza from Debonairs or Panarottis was a luxury I could only dream of. Late in the night, I cried, knowing well that it was in vain. But I kept on studying – I had promised myself that I would see this through, no matter the cost.

Sometimes, on the weekends, when fellow students invited me to go with them to expensive places, I would lie about why I could not go, to draw attention away from the fact that I could not afford it. I refused to waste what little pocket money I had. When I went to sleep on an empty stomach, I knew that, at home, my mother and grandmother were struggling, too.

Dating that year was also difficult for me. Charm would not be enough to attract an upscale UCT student. Where would I take her for a date? It was also an interesting phenomenon that, while some girls were Xhosa, Sotho or Zulu, most of the time they spoke English with just a hint of a British accent. The township boys who had not gone to the same private schools as the wealthy girls were clean out of luck.

If I thought my life at PE Technikon was difficult, I was in for a rude awakening. The great equaliser was that I lived on campus and had proper funding for my education and all the necessities, but I still had to suppress the urge to enjoy university life, and all its trappings, with abandon. Whenever I saw other students who didn't have accommodation and struggled to make ends meet, I felt sad – their struggle was also mine.

My foundation studies were also full of novel academic experiences. I still had a chip on my shoulder from my matriculation year in high school and my chapter at PE Technikon. I studied very hard, wanting to be awarded the Dean's Merit Award so that I would not have to pay the family contribution the following year. I was very involved in every class and took part in every question-and-answer session.

The foundation classes were designed to cover the five years of basic high-school music courses, or University of South Africa (UNISA) music grades required to enter a university diploma or degree course, in one year. The professors taught at a fast pace, trying to cram five years of material into only one.

Professor Davids continued to work with me on my singing as I learnt technique – singing not arias, but *arie antiche,* and doing vocal exercises again and again.

One day during a lesson, while we were warming up and singing scales, Mama Virginia, as I called her, started laughing. Astonished, I asked her what was going on.

'I'm just reminded of the day you came to sing for us in your audition, and how you've grown accustomed to our decorum now,' she responded. 'Big boy, you looked so lost and out of place then. Remember how you came with your travel bags and heavy jacket while it was so hot, and took all the baggage into the audition room?'

We both laughed, but I was embarrassed about how green I had been. I learnt, during that lesson, that the aria I had sung in my audition had been too advanced for me, but since the panel knew about my background and my lack of vocal understanding and training, they had allowed me to sing it so that they could hear what kind of voice I had.

I was so excited about studying for an hour a week with Professor Davids. I also had three half-hour sessions every week with Colin Howard, the pianist who had played at my audition. During the first half hour of my time with Professor Davids, we would work on vocal exercises and technique. Mr Howard would then come in for the second half of the lesson to accompany me on whichever songs Professor Davids had assigned me.

Professor Davids's motherly instincts, her support and intuition when something was troubling me, coupled with her ability to offer me practical solutions, drew me closer to her. All her students felt the same way – however, a select few of us would be lucky enough to claim huge portions of her heart.

Professor Davids's husband, John Davids, taught foundational music theory and a course in General Music Knowledge, a prequel to the History of Music course. Mr D, as I called him, was a staunch and strict teacher, but outside the classroom, if anyone needed extra help, he would always avail us of his time.

Mr Davids had a long history of teaching music in high schools, and he also served as an accompanist and teacher with many local choral choirs in Cape Town. He was (and still is!) the CEO of the ComArt (Community Arts) organisation in Elsie's River, a non-profit organisation that offers access to arts training and resources to promote community growth, development and nation-building.

My classmate Thato Machona, a baritone from Langa township in Cape Town, and I joined ComArt as choir members. We rehearsed with the choir every Monday evening; Mr Davids offered us transportation, and paid us for rehearsals as we became more involved with the youth segment of the organisation.

From the onset of my studies at UCT, I was exposed to the power of the arts as a tool for community development.

# Chapter 14

# The dormitory hustle

While finishing my foundation studies, I was thinking ahead and preparing for the next year of school. When I visited home that December, I found out that my Aunt Xolisiwe, who had helped me with some monthly pocket money during my foundation year, had given birth to a little boy, who was then three month old. She had named him Lihle, meaning 'the time is right'. It was a moment to celebrate, but a few days later, it occurred to me that, now that there was a baby, Xolisiwe would need to focus her attention and her finances on him. Her priorities would change. I knew I would have to hustle even more for pocket money, as it may no longer come from home.

Before Christmas, I received my final foundation-year marks. They were high, thankfully, as I had worked very hard that year. It was clear that the sleepless nights had paid off. In addition, I received the Dean's Merit Award, which paid the family contribution for the following year. Changes in my family situation incentivised me to apply for the Arts and Culture Scholarship to help with my living expenses in Cape Town.

I was also moving to an apartment-style residence the following year, having had enough of the first-tier residence and their regulated meal times – where, if you miss your time slot, you miss out on eating. Our schedule at the music college differed from the rest of the university's, so those of us who lived in residences sometimes missed our meals because we had classes or rehearsals during lunch and dinner. Even if you arrived thirty minutes before the kitchen closed, the other students had often finished the food.

I applied for a plac in Liesbeeck Gardens, where most of the other music and dance students lived. I then applied for a scholarship. Ms Dawn Madolo, who was very helpful to our local ensemble, assisted me through this process. Working with her office, I could expedite my application; by the time the new year rolled around, I was slated to receive another scholarship. Working on Mondays with the ComArt Choir in Elsie's River also came in handy for pocket money, as I went home with no less than R50 – sometimes more.

As financial-aid students who lived in apartment-style residences, we received stipends of R500 a month to aid with groceries. In that first year at Liesbeeck, I lived in a two-bedroom flat with Kenny Ganya, one of my classmates from Queenstown (since deceased).

Kenny and I agreed to combine our groceries, each contributing equally to save money. However, when the end of the month came and our stipends were deposited into our accounts, he always back-tracked from our agreement. Eventually, we were buying fewer groceries than we had planned and squandering our money on alcohol and happy-hour sessions at our favourite pub, Champs. Frivolous and irresponsible may not be sufficient to describe our behaviour that year, as we got into trouble more times than I'd like to remember.

The new year promised to be a busy and startling one at school: UCT has high academic standards, and our foundation coursework did not guarantee entry to the first-year courses. Students needed to excel in all the courses to show that they could handle the first-year academic load; so, the university expelled a few of those in my foundation class who possessed 'golden voices' but had a hard time with the related academic coursework. It was a sad moment when I realised that friends I had made the year before would not come back in the new year.

Our first-year syllabus consisted of eight courses, and they were all fast-paced. Professor Gobbato taught Italian, and Diction and Presentation, for first-year students. He was calm, patient and insightful, and his style of teaching, coupled with his vast knowledge, set him apart from the rest of his colleagues. We regarded him as a walking encyclopaedia.

However, when directing productions, he was a different person. Professor Gobbato could make any of his actors or singers give life to the character he or she was portraying. But, there were some elements he could not stand, among them stupidity and a lack of preparation and attentiveness among his singers.

'*Jesu Maria*', '*Santa Maria*' and '*Santa Cielo*' were some of his favourite expressions he uttered in your face if he was not getting what he wanted. I remember when we did *Opera Kaleidoscope*, a concert of semi-staged scenes from different operas. I was in my second year and working on a stagecraft assignment. My duty was to help operate lights and other stage equipment from the booth and backstage at the Hiddingh Campus in Gardens, close to downtown Cape Town, where UCT's Little Theatre is located. The third-years, seniors and some graduate students were the principals. In one scene, they did the last act of Puccini's *Manon Lescaut*, and one tenor could not grasp the piece. Initially, Professor Gobbato was patient with him, but nothing was coming of his efforts. Finally, he lost it.

'This is Puccini, love. This is verismo, love! It must be real! Do you understand me, love? Do you understand the meaning of your words? Do you understand this music? What are you saying, love?'

The tenor just stood there, dumbstruck, which only produced further outrage.

For Professor Gobbato, you could have an ugly voice, as long as you understood the drama and expressed the conviction. He languished at the notion of people who thought they could get away with a beautiful voice alone. He understood the opera world and the changes and requirements in the business. And he encouraged us to be more than beautiful voices and to work very hard in deriving our drama from the text, which the composer and librettist had worked at in planning the story. Amid all his tantrums, the result was always phenomenal. We all benefited from, and enjoyed, working with and learning from him.

When he worked with the principals while I was still a chorus member, I watched him and asked questions, trying to absorb as much knowledge as I could.

In our Diction and Presentation classes, he taught us how to dissect songs and arias, understanding their language construction and performances. I have seen few people in my lifetime who can move others to tears through instruction. Professor Gobbato is one of them. Among the many students he taught, he enjoyed working with Pretty Yende, who is now making waves throughout the world since her days in the La Scala Young Artist programme and her win at the 2009 Belvedere Competition. It was always refreshing to see the people motivated by what he was saying bring characters to life and excel in their performances.

When 2008 arrived, it was a chance for us newbies to join the ranks of the Opera Workshop class and perform actual roles. Professor Gobbato assigned me the role of Leporello in *Don Giovanni*, and gave me some smaller parts for the Opera Kaleidoscope programme.

At that point, I had already performed with the Cape Philharmonic Orchestra in their Youth Concerto Festival as a bass soloist for Brahms's *A German Requiem*, with the KwaZulu-Natal Philharmonic Orchestra in their Youth Concerto Festival, and as a bass soloist in Mzilikazi Khumalo's Zulu oratorio, *Ushaka KaSenzangakhona*. For these opportunities to sing with such incredible orchestras, I am thankful to Louis Hyneman and Bongani Tembe.

I had also won my first vocal competition – the Schock Prize for Singing, an annual voice competition sponsored by the Schock Foundation. The competition is open to full-time students of the South African College of Music in their second or third year of study. Coincidentally, Musa Spelman won the best female voice division – so two Musas won the competition that year!

Prior to starting Opera Workshop classes, I already had two small roles under my belt – l'Hôtelier in Massenet's *Manon* and Antonio in *Le Nozze di Figaro*. I was making strides; the blunt sword was being ground on both its edges by Virginia Davids and Angelo Gobbato.

# Chapter 15

# The ultimate gatecrasher

As early as 2008, my third year of study at the University of Cape Town, I learnt the price of being an opera singer – how the intense life of travelling and hustling can affect relationships with family, friends and loved ones. You'll recall how my relationship with Bulelwa was a prequel to how things could easily fall apart under one's nose. When my grandmother's cousin, Thembi Ngqungwana, passed away in 2007 after a long battle with illness, I could not go to the memorial service because it was tech week in our production schedule. Since then, I have missed many birthdays and other celebrations, and I have even lost more girlfriends.

That year may have been the most exciting time of my life so far, with studies and travel, but it also brought the unwelcome and painful news of the passing of my grandmother. After years of working diligently, she had fallen ill and been forced to retire. Her illness didn't seem to be a grave matter initially, so the news shattered my world and took me completely by surprise. I nearly missed that service, too.

By then, I was preparing for the role of Leporello in *Don Giovanni*, coaching with Lisa Engelbrecht, an excellent operatic coach who worked with the Opera Workshop students. She is a UCT and Royal College of Music in London alumna and holds a doctorate in music.

With Lisa, I learnt my entire role, while with Angelo my work was on recitatives.

Marcus Desando, staff director for Cape Town Opera at the time, was to direct the production of *Don Giovanni*. Kamal Khan served as the guest conductor and was scheduled to take over directorship of the Opera School after Professor Gobbato retired at the end of the year.

Kamal had been an assistant to Maestro James Levine at the Metropolitan Opera for years before becoming the resident conductor and chorusmaster at Palm Beach Opera, spreading his wings further in the opera world. He worked with us before the actual rehearsal period. He and Marcus went through production notes and concepts, and they delved into research method and preparation for each character and role.

That winter break, I didn't even get to visit home. A group of youths from ComArt was leaving for the UK on an exchange programme with Wren Music in Devon, an organisation that boasted a broad programme based on principles for developing excellence in folk-music practice, using folk music and its related disciplines to promote community development and social inclusion. The two groups planned on exchanging cultures and ideas, hoping to create a lasting dialogue.

Unfortunately, one young woman who was part of the group did not process her passport and travel details in time. Since ComArt was to receive funding for this trip, they needed to have finalised everything by a specific date. Realising that they were in a jam at the last minute, the administrators at ComArt remembered me from my work with the adult choir. Knowing I had a passport and was available, they approached me to see whether I would be interested in going on the trip with them.

## THE ULTIMATE GATECRASHER

Though I felt sorry for the girl who had been planning this trip for a long time and had even been involved with its fund-raising efforts, it was a big deal for me to be granted the opportunity. Bertha Losper, a teacher and a member of the ComArt organisation, accompanied us on the trip, as did Lorraine Isaacs, also a teacher and ComArt member.

It took eight long years before I could put my passport to good use, which was now just two years shy of its expiration date. I had wanted my passport so badly at the age of sixteen, but when I finally got it, it had seemed like a waste of money; money that I could have used elsewhere. I couldn't help but remember the disparaging remark from my schoolmate, saying that I'd never leave Port Elizabeth, let alone the Eastern Cape – and how his remark had hurt me, as it did seem to reflect my reality.

But now, here I was, on an overseas trip – in a Boeing 777, ready to depart for 'Mother England'. I was so excited; I just wished I had powers to show all the naysayers in my family and back in Port Elizabeth what was happening in my life. Somewhere in the back of my mind, Tupac Shakur's song 'Picture Me Rollin'' was playing, and I had that innate and adolescent desire to show off. Childhood memories rushed back, and for a moment it felt like I had conquered the world.

I had been on a plane only once before, on a trip to Port Elizabeth from Cape Town, to do a concert with Richard Cock and the Eastern Cape Philharmonic Orchestra at the annual Last Night of the Proms concert. While that was a novel experience, it paled in comparison to this.

The feeling of boarding an international flight, with onboard entertainment and no fewer than three meals, as Musa the student – who enjoyed the free drinks, which the flight attendants were happy to give him in abundance – was enough to set my heart beating faster. And oh, my Lord Jesus – the huge difference between the landscape there and the one in which I'd grown up? I was in awe, hearing real British English and the related accents. Remarkably, some of the designs in Cape Town, once a governorship of Britain, resembled old places like Oxford and Cambridge. I was in a First World country for the first time. While people did live on the streets there, the wealth amazed me. I had to contain it all and take it in, much like I had done when I visited Joburg for the first time with the PE Technikon Choir. Inside, however, I couldn't believe it.

We were lucky to have a fantastic flying experience and a great time teaching in the schools every weekday. We were scheduled to be in Devon for three weeks, teaching Cape Malay, Xhosa, Zulu and Sotho songs, explaining their historical background, and demonstrating our cultural dances.

What stood out the most about our new locale was the comprehensive teaching programme offered in Exeter and Devon. The schools had balanced curricula, which combined both arts and science. This was different from our backgrounds in South Africa, where no such union existed. Children of all ages, from Grade 1 to high school, took part with great enthusiasm. We started each lesson with a demonstration of one or two of our indigenous songs. Then, we continued by teaching the students one easy song. First, I'd write the lyrics on the board and recite them in rhythm, but slowly, for them to catch on.

Once the students had learnt the lyrics and the correct rhythms, we'd teach them the melody and then work the room, teaching them the dances. It was always fun teaching them these foreign songs and joyful to see how interested they were in our presentations. Each night, after our presentation, different families from members of the Wren Organisation hosted us.

They were hospitable, especially their leaders, Paul Wilson and Marilyn Tucker, and their children, Amy Wilson and Paul Tucker, who, among many other people, transported us and entertained us while we were there. Those three weeks in Devon are some of the most refreshing, pleasurable times I have had to date, and I will never forget them.

While we were there, Mr Davids, Professor Davids's husband, kept in touch with us, sending us pocket money to spend. Before we returned to Cape Town, we had time to enjoy a few days in London, where Mark Dornford-May, a British stage director now based in Cape Town, had arranged for us to see *The Mask of Zorro*, the musical, at the Garrick Theatre on London's West End. Seeing how real professionals did it live on stage, and how everything looked like a seamless process, motivated me. Now, with hindsight, I know there was an army of people backstage working double shifts to make it a reality. From the day I had seen that Sir Willard White performance as Die Sprecher, until now, seeing my first musical performed live, I was convinced that this was what I wanted, and I knew I needed to achieve it. That was it. My mind was made up to work even harder. Perhaps, one day, people would watch me on the West End too? Little did I know that the prophecy would one day be fulfilled.

We had a fantastic time in London, sightseeing and enjoying the show and the food. When we landed at Cape Town International Airport, the Davidses and other members of the organisation were waiting there to welcome us back.

Mr Davids and his wife played such a supportive role in my life. Over the years, our relationship has moved beyond that of a teacher–student and parent–child relationship to one of deep friendship.

They are among many people, including those in the ComArt community, who took care of me while I was in Cape Town. I will forever be indebted to them; it is with them that I found a home away from home, and a family. Leaving behind the only life I had known in Port Elizabeth, I didn't know how I would handle things in Cape Town. It was so far away and so foreign. But God works in mysterious ways, as always, placing angels on earth in the form of ordinary citizens who opened their homes and lives to me and made me one of their own.

Stage rehearsals awaited us on our return from our lovely trip to the UK. Of the group who had made the trip, Thato Machona and I were the only two taking part in the production of *Don Giovanni*. Gillian Lindner, coordinator of concert scheduling and performances at the music college, had approached me before I left for the UK about film-maker Roger Lucey. Lucey, then the director of documentaries for e.tv, a South African TV network, was shooting *Aria del Africa*, a film about the changing face of opera in South Africa.

The documentary would cover the lives of two young opera singers from poor parts of the country as they prepared for their first professional production. Gillian had thought of Musa Spelman, the soprano at the music college who had won the female prize at the 2007 Schock Prize for Singing, and me.

When I returned from the UK, Roger filmed our lives in our respective university residences, including our rehearsals at the music college and our music lessons with Professor Davids. He also interviewed us in the music school and at the Baxter Theatre, and planned to visit our homes in the Eastern Cape. Ms Spelman's home town was Mthatha, a city about 480 kilometres north-east of my home town.

We started the rigorous rehearsal period with Kamal, who is very finicky about musical details. With Kamal, I got a foretaste of how particular the coaching style is in North America and the Western world. He bumped heads with us on some occasions, not letting go of details and demanding a high standard of musicianship and artistry. I remember how, at first, it seemed odd that he would get upset if one of us doubled the 'm' in the Italian *m'ama* ('she/it loves me') to *mamma*, changing the meaning to 'mother'.

With hindsight, I know the difference and the significance to someone who speaks or understands Italian. It just seemed odd for his blood to boil over an 'm', as if it were the end of the world. In the greater scheme of things, there was so much going on in the world that we needed to be upset about; phrasal doubling was not on that list, I thought.

His demands and presence at UCT had a significant impact on the students' musicianship and produced singers who came to be known on the international stage – Hlengiwe Mkhwanazi, a soprano from Durban who won awards at the Hans Gabor Belvedere Singing Competition and was part of the Ryan Opera Center studio at the Lyric Opera of Chicago for two seasons; Thesele Kemane, a bass-baritone from Kimberley who joined the Juilliard School of Music in the autumn of 2014 and, in 2016, joined the studio programme of the Frankfurt Opera; and Tshepo Moagi, a tenor from Vryburg who also won prizes at the Belvedere Singing Competition.

In addition, Kamal has worked with Siyabulela Ntlale, a baritone from Port Elizabeth and fellow UCT alumnus who, in the summer of 2014, also won many prizes at the Belvedere Singing Competition and has since made many important debuts in Germany. Another singer who worked with Kamal and who is enjoying huge success in Europe is Levy Sekgapane, a tenor who specialises in the bel canto repertoire, Rossini in particular. In 2014, Levy won the Belvedere

Singing Competition in Amsterdam, in which three of the new wave of South African singers were finalists, followed by the Montserrat Caballé International Singing Competition in Spain and the Southern African Music Rights Organisation (SAMRO) Best Western Art Music Singer award. Much like Pretty Yende had done in 2011, in 2017 Levy won the Operalia World Opera Competition, founded by Plácido Domingo. He, too, is making important operatic debuts the world over.

While I was in the UK with the ComArt Youth, and then back in Cape Town to begin rehearsals, I had kept little contact with my family. From my end, it wasn't deliberate – but it turns out that, from them, it was. My grandmother had been sick for months and a family member was taking care of her, but her health deteriorated to the extent that she was taken to the emergency room and admitted to intensive care. A week later, she passed away.

No one told me.

After an intense rehearsal process, the opening of *Don Giovanni* was drawing near, and we were ready for it. However, the day before the show, I received a distressed call from home to inform me of my grandmother's passing – a week earlier.

The news came as a shock, a complete surprise. As my family informed me of her death, all I could think of was that a full week had passed before anyone had told me she had died! For months, I'd not known she had been that sick. When I'd called in the months leading up to being notified of her passing to check how everyone was doing, they had always glossed over the details of her whereabouts. During one call, when I had pressed my family for exact details, they had said she was just visiting one of her brothers and getting some well-needed rest.

As you can expect, I was more than enraged. But I kept it together during the call, saying only, 'Thank you for letting me know,' then hanging up.

At that point, my whole world seemed to fall apart. The first thing I did was buy a bottle of vodka: I feared that, if I stayed sober, I might do something irrational. My urge overrode my religious guilt about drinking.

My thoughts were still racing as I walked to the liquor store. I was livid: the audacity of my family to have hidden this most important news about my grandmother's declining health, for months!

That day, a part of me died with her, and my respect for my family members decreased. Perhaps, in their defence, they had hidden the news from me because they knew how much she meant to me, but I thought I still deserved to know. In Cape Town, I was only a two-hour flight away from her as she fought for her life. Had I known, I could at least have taken a day or two to visit her.

My mother claimed she feared what the news might do to me – after all, my grandmother had raised me and taught me about values, about life. I deserved to know. Period.

I would not let this affect the upcoming performance, though, which was important. Sitting there and crying, wishing she would come back, would not help – but performing to the best of my ability and dedicating my major debut role to her memory would, and that is what I decided to do.

I chose not to tell many people about this incident, save for my closest friends. My friend Tukela Pepeteka, who is from my home town and who was also a student at UCT, living on the same floor in Liesbeeck Gardens, joined me in my apartment to toast my grandmother's life.

The day of the performance arrived, and still I told no one else about my loss. I was still angry, but I knew that anger would affect my performance. So, I buried it and used its energy instead, by transferring it into my performance. Perhaps the fact that *Don Giovanni* is a comedy lightened the load – though, in hindsight, performing an *opera buffa* when my grandmother had just died seemed odd. Still, I could feel her spirit with me that night.

This is what a review from a local paper said of my performance: 'Opening night, however, belonged to Musawenkosi Ngqungwana as his servant, Leporello. He is a natural performer who combines dramatic excellence, as shown in his perfect comic timing with the aria "Madamina, il catalogo è questo", and effortless vocal ability, demonstrated in his fine rendition of "Ah, pietà! Signori miei"…'

The rest of the performances of *Don Giovanni* went well. I focused my energy and vented my frustrations on the stage. When I called home and asked them to book me a morning flight for the service, someone had the audacity to suggest that I take a twelve-hour bus ride to the service after my final performance on Friday night. Even if I had agreed to travelling by bus, it would have been impossible: the bus would leave at 5 p.m., but my performance only finished after 11 p.m. I thought the least they could do was pay for a plane ticket home. Surely, payment from her funeral policies could pay for a plane ticket?

Roger, the documentarian, still needed to film my home and, since most family members would be there during the funeral service, this would be an opportune time to shoot. He booked the flight and paid for it from his own pocket. We'd fly on the morning after my final performance.

On Saturday morning, Roger picked me up from Liesbeeck and we drove to the airport. When we arrived at my family's home, the viewing ceremony was over, and I did not have to see my grandmother in that helpless state. At least all the memories I have of her are happy and encouraging ones.

## THE ULTIMATE GATECRASHER

At the service, I read her obituary, but that was the extent of my participation. I did not talk to anyone until after the service. The service went well, with Roger filming it and interviewing some family members afterwards. As soon as he finished with the interviews, he left for Grahamstown, about an hour's drive east and the home of Rhodes University, as he had another project to do there.

I knew my anger was still brooding. So, without making a scene, I left my family and spent the rest of the day with Asanda Nontshinga, a good friend from high school who lived in Humewood and worked at Volkswagen South Africa as a project engineer. I returned home only on Sunday afternoon. By then, most family members had left. This made it easier for me; I didn't have to see or talk to them.

If Roger and I had found a return flight to Cape Town on the same day as the service, I would have left then. In my grief and anger, I had decided I was through with my family. I stayed for the day on Sunday; on Monday morning, Phumlani Ngqungwana, my mother's uncle who had been incarcerated on Robben Island and whom I respect, was still at my grandmother's home and was returning to East London on that day. He gave me a lift to the airport. We didn't say a word on the drive; even though I was calmer by then, he could sense that I was not in the mood to talk. And so, we said our goodbyes.

I have not been in touch with most of my grandmother's family since the funeral. I forgave my family members – and myself, in the process – because, as time went by, I came to see that staying angry would not serve me. In fact, it would only hurt me. My relationship with my family is not the same as it was before, however – nor may it ever be again.

Later in the year, when Roger had finished editing his documentary, he submitted it to Duke University and e.tv, hoping e.tv would broadcast it. Although e.tv never picked it up, Roger did several screenings all over the country, including at the South African College of Music. A considerable number of people attended the screening there, including the Davidses, Professor Gobbato, Professor Khan and Jacky Folley, my acting teacher. The teaching and administrative staff at the music college also came, as did my friends, including Mzo Daphula, Tukela Pepeteka and Mandisinde Mbuyazwe.

The screening went well, but it was tough – especially the segment about my grandmother's funeral. It was only when I visited home for Christmas for the first time since the funeral that I felt the huge void in the house: the matriarch of the family, who had carried those yearly prayers of my childhood and united the whole family, was no longer there.

My mother did her best to fill the gap and continue our Christmas morning prayer tradition. An unwanted guest, death had gatecrashed our party and disrupted our lives and the order of things – but what it could not do was diminish our joy and all the great memories of Misiwe Dorothy Ngqungwana, who will forever live in my heart. When I have difficult days, I always think of how she would have handled each situation. Thus, I follow suit, as she knew the ways of life.

*Ah Masthathu, Machisana, Ndebe, Khophoyi, Nkomo Zibomvu, Lawu, Hasa.*[*]

---

[*] The Xhosa salutations of veneration to my grandmother's clan.

# Chapter 16

# MIAGI

Before I left for the summer holiday that year, I auditioned for Robert Brooks, the executive director of MIAGI, otherwise known as Music Is a Great Investment, a South African non-profit organisation established in 2001 with support from the Department of Arts and Culture. The company's motto is 'Uniting the Power of Classical, Indigenous and Jazz'. Among the many activities that MIAGI supports is a Mentor and Protégé Programme that encourages young and talented aspiring artists. Over the years, MIAGI has offered many young musicians the opportunity to further their studies and take part in prestigious international competitions.

Included among these aspiring artists is Pretty Yende, who, in 2008, won the International Institute for Opera and Poetry (IIOP) competition. MIAGI supported her participation in the International Hans Gabor Belvedere Singing Competition in Vienna. Subsequently, Yende has won more competitions and has made important debuts across the world, including at the Metropolitan Opera in New York City, the Royal Opera House in London, the Los Angeles Opera, the Paris Opera, and elsewhere. She has also signed a recording deal with Sony and continues touring the world, doing recitals, concerts and performances.

Robert was in Cape Town to hear a select number of students

ODYSSEY OF AN AFRICAN *Opera* SINGER

from UCT sing for his organisation. He ended up selecting four of us – Golda Schultz, Sunnyboy Dladla, Mlamli Lalapantsi and me – to take part in the next leg of the IIOP competition, slated to start in Verona in early 2009. This news was not received without controversy, as some students felt overlooked and claimed favouritism.

Robert was always going to choose someone, but that it was us and not the students who thought they deserved it more created melodrama. Some singers can be resentful and brutal with their cutting remarks, saying hurtful things while expecting you to apologise for being successful. I refuse to conform to that mentality or let people define me or pigeonhole me according to their own narrow views. I live by the words of the late comedian Bernie Mac: 'Do not limit yourself. How you start is how you finish. If you let people put tags on you, you will never be able to remove them. You have to make people respect you. Respect is bigger than dollars and cents.'

This little stunt by sore losers was not going to deter me.

After Robert selected us, we went to apply for Schengen visas at the Italian consulate in Cape Town. We would audition for *Turandot*. Golda would audition for the role of Liu, and the rest of us would try out for the roles of Ping, Pang and Pong.

Professor Khan had played for our audition and coached us in what little time we had to prepare for the trip.

We took a KLM flight from Cape Town to Amsterdam and, from there, a connecting flight to Venice. There, we met the taxi driver hired by the IIOP to transport us to Verona from Venice. We tried to speak to him and asked him a question – to which his response was, '*Scusi signori, non parla Inglese* (Sorry, I don't speak English).'

The organising committee had dispatched some assistants to help us if we needed directions or any other guidance. Two of them, Laila Shaila and Francesca Riva, spoke English, but in Verona there were limits on who spoke, or was willing to speak, English. *Non parla Inglese* was the national anthem of Verona. If you asked questions in English, you seemed to offend people. I could almost see people's thoughts: 'How dare you speak to us in that language? You're in Italy! You will speak our language, period.'

In the first week, we stayed in a hotel about a twenty-five-minute walk from the Teatro Filarmonico di Verona. It was January: wintertime in Europe. This was new to us southern-hemisphere folks, who had left our summer weather back home. Now, having been in Norway and Canada during the winter, I realise that my first winter experience in Italy was a walk in the park. But, the aesthetic was all new, and it was *freezing*. Sunnyboy just hated the weather. He shivered all the time, which caused Mlamli and me to tease him endlessly. I think it's safe to say that he abided by the weather, instead of getting used to it. Importantly, just being in Italy, the birthplace of Opera, was both rewarding and humbling. Much like my first overseas trip, to the UK, this was another novel experience I had to absorb. Part of me wanted to jump for joy, but I had to keep it all in.

When we got to the theatre on the day of the first round of auditions, there were many singers, most of whom were Asian. As we waited for our turn to sing, we watched as some of the other singers passed us, looking condescendingly at us and shaking their heads, while some others warmed up as they were passing by, showing off.

In retrospect, I've learnt that this is quite a 'singer' thing to do. Whenever I go to auditions, there are always singers who show off or look at me condescendingly, while I am left wondering why they don't just go to the warm-up room.

Golda went first. She has an exquisite voice and is a smart singer. But, while she was singing 'Signore Ascolta', Liu's first aria from the opera, they interrupted her before she had a chance to reach the aria's climax.

'*Grazie,*' is all we could hear – which we interpreted to mean, 'Thank you, and let's get on with it.'

Golda knew that her chances would be slim, but she kept her head held high and understood that it was only a contest. Her later success in Europe and North America, including her debut at the Teatro Alla Scala in Milan, the Salzburg Festspiele and the Metropolitan Opera, her glowing reviews from the *New York Times* and important newspapers in the UK and Europe, and her attending the Juilliard School of Music, are a testament to her will power and work ethic. She continues breaking ground and making important house and role debuts.

The incident reminded me, again, of years ago when, with the Ultimate boys in Port Elizabeth, we had been cut off at the *Shell Road to Fame* competition. We had left defeated. Golda fared better than we had, however, and exited gracefully.

Next, it was the three boys' turn. We could feel the pressure: we had seen so many other trios auditioning for the roles of the ministers, and they had all been superb. As we were the only black trio, we feared they might cut us off too.

'Boys, let us sing for our lives! The rest depends on them and baby Jesus,' was our mantra as we prepared to enter the room.

Éva Marton, the famous Hungarian dramatic soprano known for her operatic portrayals of Puccini's *Turandot* and *Tosca*, and Wagnerian roles, led the panel of judges. They chose for us the first entrance of the ministers, 'Fermo! Che fai? T'arresta!'

If I were to evaluate our performance that day, I would say it was not a technically proficient one, but one that had gusto, heart and power, which forced everyone on the panel to listen and take note. That night, we proceeded to the next round, and we continued advancing until we won the finals. There were two winners for each category, so there would be an opening-night cast and a cover cast. The other cast comprised an Italian tenor, an Argentinian tenor and a Latvian baritone.

The powers that be announced that we were to be the cover cast, a decision that made my two colleagues livid. I remained indifferent about the situation, as the company had also offered me the small role of Il Mandarino. While my friends had been given the smaller role of Il Principe di Persia, they were not happy, and understandably so. Il Principe di Persia does not appear on stage and has only one singing line – when he is executed backstage. My role had a somewhat more significant presence in the production.

We staged our scenes. The director was very nice and spoke both English and Italian when he gave instructions. The conductor was an entirely different story and did not have a pleasant personality. From the start of the rehearsals, he never spoke to us. Instead, he sent notes through the stage manager or the director. So, it was a stressful situation, considering that conductors can make performing either a pleasant experience or a terrible one, depending on how they feel about each singer.

But then, a miracle happened. The Latvian baritone slated to sing Ping had a prior opera commitment elsewhere and had failed to communicate this information to the conductor. Thus, he missed two major orchestra rehearsals.

At first, the conductor ignored me and sang my part while rehearsing the minister's entrances, but this affected the two first-cast tenors because the trio was incomplete – they needed every chance in the limited rehearsal time. I had already sung the part of Il Mandarino. I sang it for my life, selling myself as best as I could. When the baritone returned during another orchestra rehearsal and could not sing because he had performed a Verdi opera the previous night, the conductor had to use me.

One of the tenors whispered, 'Relax, you've got this. Just sing it and do not pay attention to anything else.'

Much obliged, I sang with them and was a perfect fit, as I could listen to their voices and adjust my voice accordingly. The conductor seemed pleased and, without saying a word to me, let the stage director know that I was now in the opening-night cast. When the director told me, I was excited, but I had to contain my enthusiasm because my colleagues were still at odds with the conductor.

While I sympathised with my brothers, I knew I needed to make the most of the opportunity. Having come from difficult circumstances, I would always fight hard to get where I needed to be. But celebrating while they were being treated indifferently and unfairly seemed out of place.

Later, when we had sung our last performance, the conductor came up to me and spoke English for the first time, to my utmost surprise. Had he been able to hear us when we mumbled and cursed him out? I trembled at the thought.

'You did well,' he said, 'though you still have a lot of work to do. Continue working hard and remember to study, study, study, and never stop learning. Good luck with your future!' He patted me on the arm.

One critic said of our performance, '*Assai meglio le tre maschere, Bayempini Ngqungwana, Enea Scala e Carlos Natale (Ping, Pong, Pang) interpreti convincenti e validi cantanti.*' Or, in English: 'The three masks were much better, Bayempini Ngqungwana, Enea Scala and Carlos Natale (Ping, Pong, Pang), convincing interpreters and valid singers.'

We met many incredible singers from the competition, including

Daniel Golossov and Satomi Ogawa, who became great friends to us, showing us around and even donating their money to us when we had run out of funds to spend. I remember when, during a break from rehearsals, they took us to Venice, where we had the most fantastic time. When I needed a work permit for the production, as my visa had only been a visitor's visa, Daniel played a fundamental role by speaking Italian to the police on my behalf, facilitating everything amid the difficulty of dealing with immigration officers.

When it was time for us to part ways, Daniel and Satomi gave us some very expensive gifts and hugged us goodbye. By then, we had thrown out the window all tensions between us regarding the conductor and role assignments. Sunnyboy Dladla would go on to make strides in Europe. He later became a member of the International Opera Studio of Zurich Opera while completing a master's degree at Zurich University. He continues making important debuts in distinguished international companies like the Deutsche Oper Berlin, Oper Stuttgart, Oper Zürich and the Pesaro Rossini Festival. While Mlamli still sings occasionally, he has become a successful businessperson and family man in Cape Town.

The company paid us for our performances, which helped me get through the first few months of 2009. Despite this, money problems continued to plague my life. Before completing my undergraduate studies, just when I thought I had taken care of everything, a glitch from my summer studies in 2007 arose. Somebody in the financial-aid office had assured me that summer school would be covered, but now I was told that they had made a mistake and I would have to pay the bill myself before I could graduate.

I also needed money to pay for my graduation gown and suit. My uncle, Mncedisi Ngqungwana, came to the rescue, and Professor Khan helped obtain funding from the Mellon Foundation to cover the rest of my fees. Even on the brink of my graduation, I was running into struggles, but I was also lucky in that providence and supportive people were always there to help me.

But, amid all of this, the pleasure of having performed in Italy and in school productions over the course of the year was bittersweet. I was about to graduate, but my grandmother would not be there to share in my joy. I felt the loss immensely. She had raised me, prepared my school clothes, and been to every school meeting that was required of her during my school years, from primary to high school. When I toured with the school choir, it was she who prepared all my food and gave me spending money. She had seen me struggle after high school and when I had dropped out of PE Technikon. She had witnessed my daily trials in 2004, when I was trying to make ends meet and work my way up to the University of Cape Town. Surely, she of all people deserved to see my crowning moment.

Memories of my grandmother lingered inside me and, when they called my name in the graduation hall, all I could think of was her and how she would have been so proud. When I saw the other Xhosa students walk up to the vice-chancellor and heard their mothers ululate as a sign of traditional celebration, I wished she were there to do the same.

I also wished that my immediate family had been there when the university bestowed my degree upon me, but it was not meant to be. I think what disappointed me the most was that one of my uncles, Thami Ngqungwana – the one who worked for the Department of Trade and Industry – was not there to support me. The fact that he frequently came to Cape Town on parliamentary business but never once came to see where I lived, or asked how my studies were going and whether I needed his help, was a continual source of great disappointment.

My university career had entailed five years of intense preparation, disappointment and triumph, but I had made it nevertheless and graduated from a leading African university. Fortunately, Nonkie, my long-time friend who was working in Cape Town, and my girlfriend came to support me.

I hadn't been dating her for long, so the fact that she came to support me meant a lot. Our relationship, unfortunately, didn't last long after that, but we parted on friendly terms. She had come into my life at a crucial time, when I was making a shift from undergraduate to graduate school; there had been a lot going on that had demanded my attention. It reminded me of Bulelwa, who had come into my life when I was making my first strides as a self-employed and independent artist. I see, now, that these women had met me when critical changes were occurring in my life. Perhaps they reflected these changes, and each added something valuable, however small. I could and should have done more, but this may have altered my path.

I have been lucky that most of my relationships have ended on good terms. But there were times when I hurt people. Whether that was intentional is beside the point; the fact remains that I was emotionally unavailable. Being a theatre person – or trying to be – means living a vagabond life; there may be casualties.

Nonkie was the one constant, the person who was there through it all. The two of us never judged each other. People would come and go in our lives, but we remained glued together. My grandmother aside, I can think of no other person I would have considered family.

We went to Nonkie's place after the graduation ceremony, where we had a barbecue with some of his colleagues and his girlfriend to toast my success.

Being in the opera business can result in a very lonely life, as I learnt early on, so I know, now, how to weather whatever storms may come my way. While I missed my family's presence, not knowing the rationale behind their lack of support, I knew inside myself: *a luta continua*, the struggle continues.

Forward ever, backward never. I have not looked back.

# Chapter 17

# Valour the conqueror

If I thought that my five years of undergraduate studies were tough, or the challenges I had encountered before I went to Cape Town were difficult, then I was an idealist and in for a second rude awakening. I had lived in university residences for five years and had overstayed my welcome. If I wished to continue studying at the university, I needed to get an apartment.

I had started my honours degree, which meant that I no longer fell under the financial-aid category and Professor Khan's jurisdiction. So, funding from the Mellon Foundation was out of the question, too. I could have chosen a postgraduate diploma in music, which was a two-year programme under the jurisdiction of the financial-aid office, but I would have needed to apply for funding from the postgraduate funding office if I wanted to continue my studies. This office was on the university's main campus, operated by people I didn't know. Since I was independent of the humanities faculty and the South African College of Music, I was in a category of my own.

Before graduation, Kamal and I spoke about my future and what I wanted to do after UCT. While we discussed the different options, the AVA in Philadelphia had come up and Kamal had sent a message to Danny Pantano, who handled special events and community relations, enquiring about auditions. Danny connected Kamal with Kevin McDowell, the president and artistic director of the institution. Mr McDowell agreed that Kamal could send a video audition of several of his postgraduate students, including me.

They seemed to like me from the video audition, and Kamal sent another follow-up video of my performance as Don Profondo in *Il Viaggio a Reims*. When the school invited me to join its 2010–2011 season as a first-year resident artist, I knew that choosing the two-year postgraduate diploma would have been counterproductive, as I wouldn't have completed it by the time I left for Philadelphia.

It was unusual for the AVA to accept me based on a video audition – they had never done that before. The school has a rigorous auditioning process in which all prospective resident artists audition through several rounds and, from hundreds of auditions, the institution chooses between seven and ten students. Having heard of this rigorous process, I knew I was very lucky.

Choosing degrees and schools seemed the easy part. Now, I had to think about how to bridge the gap between graduation and the start of my AVA residency in Philadelphia in September. I needed accommodation in Cape Town from as early as January 2010 and funding to pay for all my degree courses, voice lessons and coaching, living expenses and research. I also needed to put together three recitals, one of which had to be at least a traditional forty-five-minute to an hour-long recital. I only had eight months to complete all of this and still needed to plan for the AVA, the flight to Philadelphia, accommodation there, and the $13 500 I had to raise for all of this (which was about R140 000). This was a stipulation by the Department of Homeland Security: as a foreign international student, I needed to prove that I would be self-sufficient while I was in Philadelphia and, since I could not work, I needed to have money before entering the country. In South Africa, I could buy a plot of land or build a house with that sum of money! Where was I going to get it?

This was beyond the test of my character; courage needed to be my victor and protector. After the graduation barbecue at Nonkie's place, I still had to go home, although I didn't want to. Arriving at home, I had lost the taste for dialogue and drama. I did not ask my mother why she never came to my graduation. The conditions there were enough to suggest that money could have played a role in her decision. Even though she is now working with children through her organisation, the Ngomso Youth Foundation – a non-profit organisation aimed at providing day-care services to preschool children – she is still a long way from becoming self-sufficient.

After Christmas, I couldn't rest. My mind was fidgety thinking about Cape Town. I called Nonkie and told him about the situation. I knew I needed to be in Cape Town to form ideas about my BMus Honours research, but I had neither accommodation nor funding. He agreed to let me stay with him for as long as I needed. On 3 January 2010, I took the overnight bus to Cape Town, not having a clue how I would achieve these objectives.

Over time, I've learnt that when you have a massive mountain to climb, you must break up the route into small parts and take one step at a time. Before you know it, you will probably have reached the summit. I needed to follow that mentality; the first thing I needed to do was get to Cape Town and settle in at my friend's place.

Arriving in Cape Town, I went to familiar places first. Because Nonkie was at his girlfriend's place in Strand, just outside Cape Town and close to Somerset West, I had to leave my stuff at a friend's place in Newlands, a suburb next to Rondebosch, where Lindile Kula, my close friend and Tukela's cousin, lived (the same Tukela

ODYSSEY OF AN AFRICAN *Opera* SINGER

who had toasted my grandmother's departure after I had received news about her passing). Lindile worked for Cape Town Opera's Voice of the Nation Ensemble and has been my friend since our high-school choir days in my home town. He was also one of my fellow choir members in the 2002 PE Technikon Choir that competed in Johannesburg.

After finding Nonkie, we spent a weekend catching up. I then settled down to get ready for planning. Nonkie lived in Cape Town's Philippi township, a downgrade from our respective townships back home in Port Elizabeth – but this did not matter, given that I was desperate for a place to stay. Nonkie was kind enough to provide me with a weekly bus ticket and pocket money, accommodation and food.

Mr Davids, who continued transporting me on Monday and Friday evenings after the Adult Choir and Youth Ensemble rehearsals when I was staying with Nonkie, decided that Nonkie's place was not fit for me to live in. He spoke to two members of ComArt, who had a spare room where I could be accommodated.

I was hesitant because of my pride, but I finally agreed; Ms Evadne Abrahams, a lecturer at the University of the Western Cape, and Mr Louen Kleinsmidt, a computer expert at UCT, welcomed me into their home in Belhar, a middle-class coloured suburb close to Elsie's River on the Cape Flats. Mr Kleinsmidt, Thato Machona and I were among the basses of the ComArt adult choir. I ended up staying with Ms Abrahams and Mr Kleinsmidt for about a month before funding came through from the Postgraduate Funding Office in March 2010.

They took good care of me, providing me with clothes, toiletries, bus tickets, money, accommodation, and tons of food and love, and giving me space to write and read.

For the first two months of the year, I had been hustling in all the university departments to get funding and scholarships to finance my research degree and get a supervisor. Dr Anri Herbst, an associate professor responsible for the education sector of the research department, agreed to be my supervisor. As part of my initiation into research, I took research methodology classes with Dr Morné Bezuidenhout, then the director of the South African College of Music.

My time in Philippi gave me a lens through which I could witness primary-school-aged children. The neighbourhood's poverty and the conditions that affected those children's education made me think about what I would write about in my research. By the time I had started my first class with Dr Bezuidenhout, I had already planned my rationale, hypothesis and research methodology.

Dr Herbst remarked that I worked like an ant storing food for winter. I wanted to write about poverty and education, but Dr Herbst said it was too broad a research question to pursue. Since my degree did not require this much, compared to a PhD dissertation, I needed to condense my thinking to research-essay format and focus on a specific subject within the education field.

After much debate, we decided I would research the foundation class. The final title and scope of my essay would be 'Investigating the Academic Progress of the Foundation Class at the University of Cape Town: A Case Study'. From this scope of work, I focused on a group of students, interviewing them, gathering the quantitative and qualitative materials of their course results, and then comparing those against their socio-political background, which affected the foundational education in their respective homes. From this first-hand research, I would craft case studies and draw conclusions.

With Professor Davids and Gillian Lindner, we decided on a date for my major recital at the Baxter Concert Hall, where Victor Tichart, who was an accompanist at the university, would play for me. I would do two operas, which would count as my minor recitals.

Amid these arrangements, I finally received scholarships from the Postgraduate Funding Office and I could afford to get a place of my own. After searching for accommodation, I found a place in Kenilworth, a suburb in the southern part of Cape Town, about three suburbs from Rondebosch, where the university is located. Evan Stansbury, from Ohio in the US, and Morne Botes, who is South African, were renting out a room in their house. They were lovely people, and I loved their house.

It had been over two months since my girlfriend, who had come to my graduation ceremony, and I had broken up. Around this time, I met a young mezzo-soprano, Kim Windvogel, who was a first-year student at the university. Kim lived in Lakeside, a suburb thirty minutes away from where I lived. She had started school in February, but I had not noticed her until now, as I was spending my time between the music library and main library on the upper campus of the university – and, between my research, I was working on music with Lisa, Kamal, Virginia and Victor.

The first day I saw this beautiful girl, I was taken with her and knew I had to talk to her. It turned out she had researched me through Virginia, as she was one of Virginia's students. I did not waste any time; one thing led to another, and we were soon dating. From then on, we spent almost every day together, despite our busy schedules. It wasn't the healthiest relationship, as we fought all the time. Sometimes she came into the library seeking attention while I was in my element trying to get work done. Unlike other girls I had dated, Kim was feisty, outspoken and hot-blooded like me. I had met my match. Her mother would later tell me that Kim was born during a stormy night. I'd occasionally call her 'stormy child', as her temperament reflected those conditions.

Kim's mother was a teacher and her father was a lawyer. Her sister Laura had graduated with a BA in Fine Arts from UCT. An upstanding family, they welcomed me right in. I even had time to visit Kim's grandparents in Worcester, about 110 kilometres north-east of Cape Town. Those few months with her were some of the most wonderful times I had in Cape Town.

We performed *Il Viaggio a Reims* first, in which I played Don Profondo. Following that was my major recital with Victor and, in between, Jacky Folley, my acting/drama teacher, had assisted me to set up a benefit concert. Her friend Caroline Bagley, who owns the Savoy Cabbage Restaurant in Cape Town, had agreed to let us use her place, while Professor Albie van Schalkwyk, appointed as Associate Professor of Piano and Chamber Music at the University of Cape Town in January 2009, offered his services to play for me for free.

Professor van Schalkwyk had returned with his wife, Hanna, to Cape Town after teaching for twelve years at the University of the Free State. An acclaimed pianist, Professor van Schalkwyk regularly performs on the concert stage with well-known artists, and he loves to work with young musicians to share his knowledge and passion for music with them. He is active in all genres of classical music, from orchestral music to the intimate world of art song. I was elated that a person of his calibre would play for me.

Our programme, which was about an hour long, included Mozart, Verdi, Donizetti, Brahms and Schubert, and even some Weill, Rodgers and Hammerstein, and Gershwin. Through this concert, I met Len van Zyl, the founder and chairperson of the Len van Zyl Conductors' Competition in South Africa. Len had been chairperson and CEO of the largest advertising agency in South Africa, Lindsay Smithers-

FCB, having earlier formed a partnership with Foote, Cone and Belding (FCB) in the US.

In the early 1990s, Len had run the Philadelphia operation of FCB as president and CEO. While living there, he had befriended several people, including Allan Schimmel and his partner, the late Reid Reames. They were all members of the First Presbyterian Church at 21st and Walnut streets together. Len wanted to keep in touch and introduce me to his friends in Philadelphia so that I would have people to show me the ropes there.

After the concert, I auditioned and received further funding in the form of the WBHO/Jan Kaminski award, facilitated by Cape Town Opera. Again, Kamal played for me. Christine Crouse, then the artistic director of Cape Town Opera, and financial director Elise Brunelle were instrumental in further supporting me.

In addition, I received funding from the National Arts Council of South Africa (NAC). That funding, along with the WBHO scholarship, the cash from the benefit concert and a private donation from another of my drama teacher Jacky Folley's friends, constituted the rest of the cash I needed to reach my goal, as the AVA would provide a monthly stipend to cover rent for all the academic months, excluding summer break.

Now, the only things standing between me and Philadelphia were my minor recital and another competition – the 29th International Hans Gabor Belvedere Singing Competition in Vienna, Austria.

# Chapter 18

# The changing tides

MIAGI's Robert Brooks had come through for me again. Of those who auditioned in Cape Town for the 29th International Hans Gabor Belvedere Singing Competition, for which Kamal again played, soprano Nozuko Teto, also a graduate student at UCT, and I made it through as candidates to compete in Vienna. My friend Luthando Qave, who at the time was in Germany, planned on joining us. The three of us would represent South Africa.

Luthando had just graduated from Operahögskolan, the University College of Opera, in Stockholm, Sweden. He was getting ready to move to the US, where he would join the Lindemann Young Artist Development Program at the Metropolitan Opera. Nozuko had been earmarked to join the Accademia Lirica di Mirella Freni in Modena, Italy, after finishing her postgraduate studies.

Following music preparations with Virginia and Kamal, Nozuko and I flew Emirates via Dubai. In Austria, Ingrid Hedlund, an Austrian native representing MIAGI, met us. Ingrid split her time between Europe and South Africa. Through her connections, we got accommodation in one of her friends' apartments, and Ingrid showed us the city and the competition venue.

The rehearsals with pianists took place at the University of Music and Performing Arts in Vienna, about six minutes west of the Vienna

State Opera. The place where we would be competing, the Wiener Kammeroper, is another six minutes south of the university. Between these institutions is a vibrant tourist town, full of life and activities.

We passed by the beautiful St Stephen's Cathedral of the Archdiocese of the Catholic Church in Vienna on our way to the competition after we had finished rehearsing with our pianists. This is one of the most recognisable buildings in Vienna, and it is full of tourists going to and fro. All these historic and cultural European buildings I was getting to see in my travels blew me away.

Arriving at the Kammeroper, we reunited with Luthando. There were many judges on the panel, including Holger Bleck and Isabella Gabor, the general managers of the competition, and various directors of opera companies, conductors, stage directors and artist agents. Some philanthropic audience members surrounded them.

When my turn came, I sang 'Madamina, il catalogo è questo' from *Don Giovanni*. By then, this aria had become a staple of my audition pieces. I had first learnt it in 2008, when I prepared for the role of Leporello, and it had become my go-to aria whenever I felt unsure and nervous. Starting with it proved fruitful; by the time I sang my second aria, 'Vous qui faites l'endormie' from *Faust*, I was comfortable and confident that I had sung well.

After the three of us had had our turns to sing, we went out to have lunch and then came back to see who had advanced to the next stage. The results were posted on a noticeboard behind a big sheet of glass. Luthando and I had progressed, but Nozuko, unfortunately, had not made it in the opera round. However, those who had registered for the operetta portion still had another chance to display their talent and perhaps win some prizes. Nozuko still sang in the operetta round.

Luthando and I began preparations for the next rounds and

ended up advancing to the finals. Each round was difficult for me, though it did not seem difficult for Luthando, who sang a famous aria with ease from *Il Barbiere di Siviglia* titled 'Largo al factotum' as if it did not have difficult high notes.

We did not win any of the first three major prizes in the finals. To be honest, this wounded my pride. As a Leo, I have the pride of a lion and I don't like losing. With hindsight, I now know how each singer feels when it doesn't go his or her way in a competition, because of our general naivety and sense of entitlement.

Luthando and I received special prizes. Luthando received an opportunity to perform in Germany and an invitation from Diane Zola, Director of Artistic Administration at the Houston Grand Opera, to join its studio programme. But Luthando had already signed on to join the Lindemann Young Artists programme in New York, so that wouldn't work for him. I ended up receiving a prize from the German newspaper *Die Zeit* to perform in two operas with the Wiener Kammeroper, but, unfortunately, I would have to turn those down when they conflicted with *Don Giovanni* at the AVA.

As a first-year resident artist at the AVA, it would be difficult to get a release to perform elsewhere. After the competition, I met different agents. One offered me a chance to audition for Raimondo in *Lucia di Lammermoor* for the Deutsche Oper am Rhein in Düsseldorf, Germany. I also had to refuse that because it conflicted with my school schedule – and, at the time, I was not ready for such a big role.

Luthando couldn't stay for the gala in Baden, Austria, where we would perform with the Wiener Kammeroper Orchestra. I remained for the gala and related rehearsals, and stayed in accommodation provided by the company. I also had many opportunities to tour the city and see two operas at the Wiener Staatsoper.

The Wiener Staatsoper – along with the Metropolitan Opera in

New York City, the Teatro alla Scala in Milan, the Royal Opera in Covent Garden, the Paris Opera and the Bavarian State Opera in Munich – is one of the grandest opera houses in the world. Performing at the Wiener Staatsoper opera house is a dream for every opera star or singer. As the cherry on top, all performances are accompanied by the orchestra of the Wiener Staatsoper, whose members also make up the Vienna Philharmonic Orchestra, one of the top orchestras in the world.

The theatre's central box gives a picturesque view of its horseshoe-shaped auditorium, with its red, ivory and gold colours. Separating the audience from the stage is an iron curtain. I could not afford to buy tickets there, but a patron of the competition had offered to do so for me.

I was fortunate to see a performance of the late Johan Botha, the acclaimed South African tenor. When I used to visit Monica Oosthuizen in PE while hustling there with Nonkie, she often played us a 2001 recording of Johan singing Italian arias. That I would see him perform live only six years later was incredible.

Some places' popularity can be overblown and overrated, but not this theatre – everything there is just top-notch and classy. I was dressed in a suit and tie, and the Vienna audience was dressed stylishly. I'll never forget those two performances. When I saw Johan perform, I was, for a moment, entranced, trying to visualise myself perform on that stage too. That image is still carved in my memory and I hope that, one of these days, it will become a reality.

After the performances and all the lovely time exploring the city, I returned to Cape Town, but not before flying back into Dubai, where the Arab immigration officers, wearing all white since it was close to the month of Ramadan, made fun of me. One of them wanted me to pronounce my last name over and over, as he could not believe the sound of it. He even called about five more of his colleagues to hear it. I was the comic relief for the day.

It did not help that my face looked younger and thinner in my passport photo than I was at the time. After this airport delay, I slept over in a hotel provided by Emirates airlines, since it was such a long layover.

The next few months after my return from Austria took a toll on my personal life. My girlfriend Kim got very emotional, and I wasn't equipped to handle that. She had known before we started dating that I would be leaving for the US in September, and she had seemed okay with us dating despite this knowledge. She had claimed she would be able to handle it when the time came for me to leave. However, I should have known that women call for a lifetime of study, requiring us to read between the lines and sometimes play a guessing game that we will never master.

Kim and I fought a lot in the days leading up to my departure. She wanted me to make promises that I knew I could not keep, not knowing what waited for me in the US. I didn't want to mislead her. In my third month in the US, I knew I needed to end our relationship.

The time difference and mismatch of schedules made it so that I didn't have the luxury of Skyping or communicating with her very often. The content of our conversations changed and everyday things, which we had once enjoyed talking about, became uninteresting. Hearing what people were doing in Cape Town felt out of place while I was trying to figure out Philadelphia and the US.

Not knowing when I would visit home again, or what I would do on finishing my studies, added to the demise of our relationship. Kim expected that I would go back to Cape Town when school was over and we would live happily ever after, while I knew that, if I ever wanted a career in this business, living in Cape Town would be neither workable nor conducive: it is too far from Europe and America. I felt that, as hard as it would be, ending the relationship then was the best decision.

Another struggle I had was leaving Cape Town itself, where I had made strong friendships and where my adopted families lived. I keep in contact with the important people in my life, but I am afraid it has turned out that I have lost touch with some folks. However, I know that this is the price of striving for success. The higher you go, the lonelier it gets. Somebody once said to me, 'If you climb a mountain, make sure you bring warm clothes, tools, a tent and blankets so that you can weather the storms.'

I *can* say that this business is not for everyone. Some people just cannot take the amount of time it requires you to spend alone, losing friends or significant others. While you are trying to make your career work and going for auditions, others are on a different timetable and are ready to settle down, knowing that their line of work provides stability and they can measure time and plan accordingly.

As an opera singer, there is no way of knowing when you might be free. Sometimes, you are not sure until that gig and its contract come in, which could coincide with your significant other's vacation or other important plans.

Age thirty is when people often reflect on their priorities, think about starting a family and make important life choices. While we as opera singers want that for our lives, too, some of us at that age and beyond are still only starting out in this business. We are still trying to build our reputations, get jobs and save enough for retirement, houses, trust funds and life's essentials – which is easier when you had the means in the first place, but it is always an uphill battle for those of us who started out in poverty.

Some have integrated career and family and make it work for them, as have some of my friends. But, for the rest of us, it is something we would rather take one day at a time.

My last performance in Cape Town was the title role in *Le Nozze di Figaro*, which had immense success. Hlengiwe Mkhwanazi was my Susanna, Nozuko Teto the Countess, and Mandisinde Mbuyazwe the Count. I concluded my Cape Town chapter in style, leaving a few days after the last performance.

Virginia and John Davids, and my girlfriend Kim, came with me to the airport. It was an emotional time, and to this day I keep in contact with all of them. Whenever I visit Cape Town, Virginia and John are among the first people I see, as well as the ComArt community, UCT staff, Len van Zyl and my other friends.

Cape Town will always be my second home. It has given me so much, for which I will be forever grateful.

# Chapter 19

# The Academy of Vocal Arts

The AVA played a vital role in putting me on the map. Coupled with my determination to succeed, it helped shape my career and pushed me to even higher levels of vocal ability. Institutions like the AVA are important, as they challenge you to become a critical thinker who is aware of their surroundings. In addition, they teach you what your body and voice can and cannot do. Sometimes, these kinds of challenges hurt your feelings – or even break your spirit – but only because we are human, and no one is perfect.

Over the years, the Academy's music staff has imparted knowledge to promising students, equipping artists with an ability to review their own performances, knowing that things could turn out a different way on stage. AVA alumni perform all over the world. In America, at any important vocal competition, AVA singers are always among the prize winners.

From studying at the AVA, I learnt that a wonderful, secure singing technique is not an attribute that develops overnight. You need patience and to let things happen in their own time. A younger soprano, starting college in 2014 when I was graduating from the AVA, asked me how long it had taken me to get to where I was then. The answer was a long time – over ten years of studying – and I continue working.

## ODYSSEY OF AN AFRICAN *Opera* SINGER

In my first two years at the AVA, while working with a new teacher, Dr William (Bill) Stone, and other coaches to learn my craft, I tried out for competitions and auditioned for companies. However, I never got a single callback or won a single prize, except for an encouragement award from the Metropolitan Opera National Council Auditions (MONCA) District Auditions in Washington, DC. A judge of one of the competitions I failed to win wrote a note that said I had a good voice but that I needed to work more on my technique, legato and understanding of my craft. I will admit that sometimes I was very disappointed, eagerly awaiting phone calls or emails for callbacks, and none came. It took me a long time to step back and say, 'I will try again next year. Meanwhile, I'll work on improving my skills.'

For two years, when nothing happened, I got frustrated – and even felt wounded, as my ego and pride were at stake. I also learnt that many vocal competitions in New York work differently from what I had grown accustomed to by taking part in European vocal competitions.

In Vienna and Verona, for example, you sang on a day and, after a few hours, the jury posted the names of those who had progressed to the next round on the venue's noticeboards. If your name wasn't on the board, you knew you'd been unsuccessful in the competition, and you could move on.

But New York thrives on suspense. Most vocal competitions have the first singer start at 10 a.m., with the last singer performing at 5 p.m. By the time the last entrant has performed, the jury has already decided on potential winners and the ones who are going through to the next round. However, they don't post results on noticeboards; instead, they call the winners. If you don't get a call, you haven't made it through to the next round. They always promised to call the singers by 7 p.m. – but not everyone would get a call, and some would only be called the following day.

The suspense of not knowing was one of the most aggravating parts of the process. While friends were celebrating getting callbacks and asking you if you'd received one, you could sense that nothing would happen in your favour; it was quite a mind trick. When – if – I received the judges' comments about why I hadn't made it, I'd feel defeated.

Those two years were horrible. I could have stayed in that safe zone, where I shifted the blame and thought the world revolved around me, but I knew I had to swallow my pride and take the criticism. Even though it may have been subjective, there was always a grain of truth in it.

As a young singer, I completed many auditions, and I will continue to audition. With luck and hope and the immense support of my manager, I have secured many jobs. I have also attended standard auditions, where people were considering me for future roles. I continue to ride the waves and present myself to the best of my ability.

Philadelphia, still my current home base, is a musical city with many patrons who contribute a lot to the arts, ensuring that it continues to exist and grow. I will forever be grateful to them for their support and encouragement.

At the AVA, I benefited from many hours with vocal coaches and music director Maestro Christofer Macatsoris. He pushed my limits; while his approach and way of doing things may not have been to my liking sometimes, I know how much I have learnt and gained from him.

It was while working with him on an almost daily basis that I understood what Kamal was focusing on back in Cape Town, when his blood seemed to boil when we would double the 'm' in *m'ama* or *madama,* and I felt that doing so didn't warrant such frustration on his part. Maestro Macatsoris expressed himself with similar mannerisms and, to me, he was an OCD-on-steroids kind of conductor. He made working with Kamal, with all his tantrums and nitpicking ways, look like child's play. This gentleman would sometimes spend an hour on a single page of music, while lambasting the resident artists about their lack of focus on and appreciation of the music. There was always a great semblance of truth to his assertions, however: we were students in our twenties, having nowhere near the level of dedication and understanding that he possessed.

In the winter of 2012, Maestro Macatsoris and I worked on the role of Sancho in Massenet's *Don Quichotte.* The school was on winter break between 20 December and 2 January and, since I never visited South Africa then (because the breaks were always too short and it was terribly expensive), I always opted to stay in Philadelphia. And so, when he asked who would be in Philadelphia and keen on working, I volunteered.

The school building was quiet and felt like a deserted warehouse. I had agreed to coach with the maestro and so, there we were, on Christmas Eve, rehearsing *Don Quichotte*. The only lit-up room in the entire school was his coaching studio, Room 20.

French music was not my forte, and *Don Quichotte* is not an easy opera to get right. I was struggling and asking myself why I had volunteered to be screamed at for three hours by a seventy-eight-year-old man on this cold and dreary Christmas Eve.

In the middle of the session, I was tempted to leave – just quit and go back to South Africa. *Why am I here?* I was thinking. *I could be at home, having soup or a hot toddy and watching movies and even calling someone up and trying to mend a broken relationship. But no, instead I'm here with this old man screaming at me because I cannot get the French words right. In the greater scheme of things, and with all the holiday celebrations taking everyone home to their families, what's wrong with me?*

I must be a sucker for punishment, because I never expressed how I felt – mostly, I think, because of my respect for him, because of his age and stature and my discipline in following decorum. It is moments like those where you show character: when things are not working as you'd like them to, and when it's easy to just revert to the familiar. Acting like I was still back in Zwide would have cost me a scholarship; I'd have made a speedy return to South Africa and to its normal: poverty and scarcity.

So, I suffered in silence, knowing there was no way to get anything right at that moment, because I was upset. We skipped Christmas Day, but worked on Boxing Day and 27 December until we got it right, as the maestro had more patience working individually with me than working with a group. That training became invaluable later, when I worked with temperamental conductors.

I could always count on Luke Housner, one of the vocal coaches at the AVA, to teach me any role, walking me through the steps until I knew it off by heart. Luke can sight-read anything, and I loved his kind and patient demeanour. He was always willing to take the extra time to teach me my roles.

David Lofton and I worked a lot on oratorios, sacred music and other roles. He challenged me on vocal technique and urged me to focus on easy singing. He also became a big brother to me, connecting me with important African-American intellectuals, artists and opera buffs in the Philadelphia region. I enjoyed David's New Year's Eve parties and many cookouts. He has stories for days and his insights into many societal and historical subjects are unparalleled.

Danielle Orlando stressed the bel canto style of singing and made each resident artist aware of what the real world required from rising artists. She challenged artists to learn a lot of repertoire so that we would be ready at any time if somebody came knocking, looking for candidates for a role or production. Like all the women who have played a fundamental role in my life, she is a strong, independent and multitalented woman.

Richard Raub always pushed me to be innovative. He made me aware of the choices I was making and taught me how to separate myself from the rest. He also played for many of my auditions and took time out of his weekends to play for my recordings.

These musicians worked so that each artist could showcase his or her specialities to the best that he or she could offer. Thor Eckert, who had worked as an artist manager and a critic and seen many productions at the Met and elsewhere, was the professional development coach at the AVA. He had the expertise to point out things that the people in casting may not like when you present.

I studied vocal singing with Dr William Stone for four years. As a voice teacher, he further developed in me what Virginia and I had started in Cape Town. He challenged me and, even though in the beginning I was always opposed to criticism and only wanted praise for my beautiful singing, he took things from that level and added aspects that have opened my voice and my high notes. My singing has improved since we worked together.

Bill also stressed the use of bel canto and natural singing, so that one could sing healthily and have a longer career. All the coaches at the AVA – despite having different approaches and temperaments – stressed the need for bel canto singing for a vocally healthy life. The bel canto style refers to the Italian vocal technique and styles of the late 1700s to the early 1800s, which emphasise the beauty of sound and a method of singing musical lines smoothly and evenly –

what we call legato, a carried sound with no glitches, much like changing gears with ease. It is every singer's goal to master this art of singing and apply bel canto ('beautiful singing') to any style or language of music.

While I didn't take voice lessons with him, I'd be remiss if I didn't give a special mention to Mr William Schuman, aka Bill – a famed singing teacher from New York City, who has been teaching at the academy for over twenty-five years. We called him a tenor specialist, as most of the tenors he has taught continue to conquer the world stages and are regulars in Vienna, London, Berlin, New York and Paris – as are his sopranos and other voice types. He also subscribes to the principle of beautiful and exciting singing.

The coach I worked with the most, and with whom I have continued working, is Laurent Philippe. Laurent is from Normandy in France, and I hated him the first time I worked with him. Laurent was vocal about my weight; whereas all the coaches had pointed this out to me before, he was not subtle about it.

From my very first coaching session, which was at 10 a.m. only two days after I had arrived in Philadelphia, he challenged and pushed me. This would become a recurring theme until he saw results. He likes to push buttons to see how his students react.

'You are doing well, my beautiful black rhino,' he said to me one day, to see how I would react.

I wanted to end him right there, while he was looking at me, smiling devilishly and testing my patience. To this day, we still butt heads when we work: my half-Zulu temperament comes out and clashes with his French temperament.

Laurent and Danielle recommended me to Bill Guerri of Columbia Artists Management Inc. (CAMI), my current manager, and the Washington National Opera. Laurent regularly works with Joyce

El-Khoury, Michael Fabiano, Ellie Dehn, Bryan Hymel, Patrick Guetti, Corinne Winters, Shelley Jackson, Chloe Moore, Sydney Mancasola and many others who have made important debuts at the world's top opera houses. When the two of us are in Philadelphia between our travels, or in the same city, such as London or Washington, DC, we also schedule coaching sessions to prepare for my upcoming roles and to ensure that I still sing on my breath with ease.

Laurent commented that I had a commanding presence and that he thought my voice was remarkable, but he stressed that it was my responsibility to achieve the total package. To this day, he and other coaches adopt this mentality: if you like singing and it is a hobby, perhaps you should not be concerned about what people say to you. However, if you are serious about embarking on a successful opera career, you cannot limit yourself and must listen to what others have to say.

I was lucky to attend the AVA, where, through their recommendations, I received opportunities to sing for people in places where other singers have not. My signing with Columbia Artists opened up even more of these opportunities.

After spending four years at the AVA, a very difficult and critical school where people do not hold your hand, I understand that I have a responsibility not only to work at my craft but also to work on my body, so that I will be presentable. In the past, opera companies hired singers because of their talent and the sheer power of their performances and interpretations. But the tides have turned, as the industry also now stresses the importance of looking the part. We young singers, unfortunately, have no say in it, and our work is to bridge the gap and work on achieving what is required of us.

In Cape Town, they praised me for having a beautiful voice. My weight, which came up sometimes, was secondary to what my voice could do. But in America, for four years, I faced constant criticism about both my singing and my weight. Having a beautiful voice alone does not cut it. More is required of you. I now realise that everything I have been through was necessary to prepare me for the real world, where sometimes people may say nothing but thank you after an audition, leaving you to wonder why you have not heard from them, even months later.

I had to realise that I was not the only voice around, and that I was rank and file with so many other talented voices around. Constructive criticism was important in making me a better singer and a more unique artist. If you want a successful career in the opera or theatre worlds, you must address these issues and understand that criticism is a part of the performing arts.

While I was still an undergraduate student, University of Michigan Professor George Shirley, on his visit to Cape Town with Associate Professor Daniel Washington, said, 'You've got to work on everything you can work on within your power, so that when you present yourself, nobody has any excuse not to hire you.'

You cannot change who you are or where you come from, but you can work on your presentation and how you want people to view you. It was hard to get through some days, but I have benefited from those experiences as an individual. Just like swords and diamonds, which need to go through fire and water to come out sharp, beautiful, shining and valuable, so we are as singers.

It is important for singers to choose a team of people they trust – a team comprising singing teachers and coaches who know their voices and will give them balanced feedback.

My philosophy is to take it a day at a time and continue working hard. From the African townships, I have come a long way; if I could break free of those inhumane conditions and make it this far, I can rise to the limits of my talent. You can do likewise – believe in yourself and listen to what people say, but filter the information you receive. Keep what you need and what works for you. Everyone has an opinion; you cannot let every opinion divert you from your objectives.

# Chapter 20

# Battling red tape

The average South African lives on a maximum of two dollars a day. Many live on less. For a long time, I was among them. That is the level of poverty I come from, a rolling circle that took many laborious efforts to escape from. Looking back on those days, I realise how fortunate I am to have been given the gift of my education and to enjoy the successes I am having in my career.

The prospect of America, and of starting a new life there, was one that excited me. I sensed that the tides were changing in my favour. Much like I had felt when I left Port Elizabeth, first for Pretoria and then for Cape Town, I sensed that America would bring a welcome change of pace. What I might not have foreseen was that it would take me a long while to get out of that cycle of poverty, even having moved to a new country.

Since I have been in the US, I have had the tremendous fortune of support from many people and organisations – including Allan Schimmel and his partner Reid Reames, who, unfortunately, passed away in June 2017 after a seven-year battle with Alzheimer's disease. When I met Allan and Reid through Len van Zyl at the benefit concert at the Savoy Cabbage in Cape Town, I found a family away from home. I was sad to miss Reid's memorial service, as it coincided with a weekend full of technical and orchestral rehearsals for the Glimmerglass Festival's production of *Porgy and Bess*.

Through my intermittent presence in their lives, I watched their strong love grow each day. Allan was fully committed to helping Reid and making him as comfortable as possible as he went through the stages of this terrible disease for seven long years. While we expected the end to be near, it's something we could never accept.

Memories of Reid Reames, of how kind and charitable he was to me and to others, are what I'll always treasure. I recall a few years back, when Allan asked Reid whom he wanted to have as a guest at his birthday dinner. Despite his illness, which challenged his memory, Reid remembered me and explicitly asked that I celebrate his birthday with them. I'm forever grateful to them for their boundless generosity.

It was through Allan that I met Andrew Senn, music director of the First Presbyterian Church in Philadelphia. From my sophomore to senior year at the AVA, I took part in the Chancel Choir of the First Presbyterian Church, and I am thankful to Andrew, the choristers, the congregation, its pastor Jesse Garner and its former associate pastor Mindy Huffstetler, who is now a senior pastor at a church in New Jersey.

As a foreign national, I could not work in the US. This presented unique challenges – while I had a full scholarship to the AVA and a monthly stipend, including the money I'd had to raise before coming to the US because of Homeland Security's stipulations, those funds were not even close to covering the actual cost of being a singer.

Going to New York City for auditions costs an average of $100 each day; if you had to go three or four times in a month, the cost became insurmountable for someone who wasn't even allowed to work.

The only thing I could do to make some pocket money was to take on a work-study programme. I could either work on campus or take a church job, which the school allowed. Church jobs provide much-needed pocket money, but also the opportunity to deal with a lot of music and sight-reading, which serves a dual purpose, as it teaches young singers the ability to learn music quickly.

For three of the four years I was at the AVA, I worked at the church every weekend. The money was paid to the school, and the school provided credit to me as a work-study student. If it weren't for that programme, I have no idea how I would have survived. Each weekend, pay was $110; whenever I could attend all rehearsals and services, I earned $440 each month. This helped me with auditions and other unforeseen bills. I was lucky that I didn't need to go to the ER for anything, because I had no health insurance, nor could I afford it then!

When graduation day dawned in May 2014, I was excited about the prospect of leaving school, but I was also stressed about what would follow. I felt a sense of déjà vu, remembering what I had felt like when I graduated from UCT in 2009, not knowing how I would pay for my honours degree and a place to stay, or how I would live.

Now that I was out of the AVA, there would be no more scholarship cheques coming my way. While I knew that my first job would be in September with the Washington National Opera at the Kennedy Center, I wouldn't get paid until after the first performance in October – five months away. How was I going to pay rent from June to August, when my lease ended?

To complicate matters further, on 19 December 2013, following the death of former South African president Nelson Mandela, I was approached by Opera Africa, a company based in Johannesburg, to perform in a newly commissioned opera celebrating his life, called *The Struggle*. Sandra de Villiers, CEO of Opera Africa, was working with South African composer Neo Muyanga to produce the work, scheduled to be performed in June 2014. I was even planning to miss my AVA graduation, since I would need to be in Johannesburg to rehearse as early as May 2014.

Opera Africa's artistic director Hein de Villiers discussed the terms of the contract with my manager Bill Guerri. While the money wasn't US-fee-based, but South African, it would still be enough to cover my rent for the summer months and carry me through until I got paid in DC at the end of October.

Doing an opera about Mandela was very interesting. Sandra had even hinted at a possible collaboration with a US-based festival after the world premiere in Johannesburg. I thought it was a great idea to delve into this work and then perhaps have time to perform it in the US.

According to our agreement, Opera Africa would wire me 5 per cent of the fee, so that I could pay for the coaching and preparation of the role. However, I never got the music. Bill and I wrote much correspondence to Opera Africa about when we might expect to receive it.

In December 2013, they told us that the composer was working on the score with a libretto in Zulu with some English interwoven, and that the piano version would be available soon. I thought that by the end of February 2014, perhaps, we would get the music. I had written to Sandra to let her know that I had productions at the AVA between February and May, and that I needed the music as soon as possible so that I could plan my life accordingly.

I was feeling apprehensive after waiting for so long, especially for new music. After sending her and her assistant, Lesiba Mogolane, several emails, Sandra finally responded on 11 February 2014:

Dear Musa,

The opera was finished last week, the team is busy with revisions, and we will be able to give you an indication when to expect your music as a matter of urgency. In the meantime, our artistic director asked me to assure you that the music is not avant-garde and should not be difficult to learn. Seeing that it is a one-act opera of plus/minus one hour shared by the rest of the ensemble, it is also not as intimidating as a full-length opera.

We responded to Mr Guerri on Monday 3 February and are waiting for his response to allow us to finalise the contract. I will then forward the final libretto as well. We are looking forward [to] meeting you in person and wish you all the best till we see you.

Regards,

Mrs D

Bill was in Europe during this time and, when he came back, we looked at the contract and signed it. On 25 February, I wrote to Mrs D, and we continued correspondence about other important matters, such as publicity photos.

On 7 March, Mrs D emailed me and Sipho Fubesi – a tenor and fellow UCT graduate, also contracted to perform in the opera – about further updates to the music and libretto.

Dear Musa and Sipho,

Hope you are both keeping well. Here is a brief update of developments:

Attached is the libretto that correlates with the orchestral score we received on Sunday, which should give you insight into the work. The composer has written the score, but, as with all new works, it is constantly revised to address amendments we asked for before it is in the public domain.

As planned, the duration of the opera is 1 hour 15 minutes comprising singers, dancers, and a children's choir.

Re the score: we will forward a vocal score asap; or if possible, the full score until the vocal score is in final form.

Wishing you all the best and we look forward to your arrival.

Warm regards, Mrs D

I wrote back, thanking her for the libretto and stressing that I understood that revisions are the norm with all new works and that I knew that this required patience. 'For me,' I said, however, 'I will appreciate even the full score whenever it may be possible to start working on the music within my schedule and then of course when the vocal score is done, I can then take it to my coaches…'

I wrote to her again on 22 March to check if she had received the signed contract. In that email, I also copied the composer to request that he send me whatever portion of music he may have finished writing by then, so that I could learn the music and familiarise myself with the style and form: 'Understanding the nature of new music and the need for revision, I am also bearing in mind that we are at the end of March, leaving us with only a month to learn, memorise and acquaint ourselves fully with the music. Noting my current schedule, I'd prefer to have sufficient time…'

I never got a response from her or the composer, although her assistant Lesiba wrote to me on 27 March that Mrs D wanted to have a Skype meeting the following day. He requested my Skype name and the best time to have this meeting, since they were six hours ahead of me in Johannesburg. But, on the 28th, at 9:10 a.m. Eastern Time, he sent me a message requesting that we move the meeting to next Monday, 31 March, because of last-minute meetings. I was getting nervous.

A whole month of correspondence had gone by with no money wired nor music sent, and we only had a month left before rehearsals were due to start on 5 May. I sensed that something was wrong.

We had the Skype meeting the following Monday and, as I had feared, the production was being postponed because of a delay in funding from the National Department of Arts and Culture. Now Opera Africa was thinking of a slot from 8 February 2014 until the end of March 2015. She asked that we defer our contract to that slot.

The problem was that, during that time, I was contracted to finish the last performance of *Carmen* in Norway and then start rehearsals for Strauss's *Guntram* with the Washington Concert Opera from 23 February to 1 March. My manager made it clear in an email correspondence that I would lose $5 000 if I were released from the DC contract. He asked if Opera Africa could increase my fee so that I could make up for the lost income for the cancelled engagement.

To Mrs D's credit, she wrote back to my manager on 17 April.

> Great news, I hope it works out. Yes we can definitely renegotiate, I will ask our artistic director to contact you. Our office is closed next week but he will liaise with you not later than 29 March.
> Wishing you a blessed Easter,
> Regards Sandra

It's safe to say she meant 29 April, since Easter was on 20 April that year.

But then that was the extent of our communication; we never had further discussions after the Easter holidays. I was very anxious. I hadn't negotiated the contract – my manager had. While we understood the contract had provisions for a reasonable postponement or cancellation, it would still need to be by mutual agreement. This meant that the settling of the deferred contract was left unfinished –

and this pained us. While I desperately needed the money, we decided that what would potentially be my debut after finishing school would not be marred by legal disputes or drama.

We had ignored other job prospects for the benefit of the Mandela opera, but then it never happened. I'm glad that I stalled the many patrons from Philadelphia and New York City who had wanted to book flights and accommodation to come see me perform in the Mandela opera.

Unfortunately, this sort of situation is not unique to only me. Many singers in South Africa find themselves in a bind, with companies and producers not handling their end of the bargain. I understand that, for most of these companies, it does not happen out of spite or ill will, but rather poor planning. People plan productions or concerts, negotiate contracts (sometimes verbally) and hire artists before securing funding. They then rely on the lottery or other government subsidies, which, even though some eventually happen, often don't come through at the hoped-for time. Sometimes, as was in Opera Africa's case, the government department can decide to withdraw their funding pledges in favour of other projects. This leaves singers, musicians, other artists, and sometimes even the companies, stranded.

It was too late for me to find another job. I was at the AVA, graduating and back to square one, having to figure out how I would get through the next five months with no tangible dollars to my name.

The first thing I did was to talk to my landlord, asking her to release me from my contract at the end of June. I put the last $1000 I had towards my bills and rent, and was left with nothing.

Allan Schimmel had become like family to me. After I'd relayed my quandary to him, he told me I could stay with him until autumn, when I would get paid from a competition I had won in New York and then move in with friends of mine from the AVA, Mackenzie Whitney and Galeano Salas.

In August, I moved to Allan's place and stayed with him until September, when my friends and I moved into our three-bedroom apartment, where I now only paid $500 a month. Allan covered that for me until I got my cheque from the competition. With that money, I could secure a place to stay in Washington, DC, for my debut with the Washington National Opera and still have some spending money to get me through until I got paid for that.

Through grace and angels – people in my everyday life – I could avert yet another disaster. But this experience reminded me that I had not quite escaped poverty yet. I was still living from pay cheque to pay cheque and, while I was saving as much as I could, I still lacked financial savvy and full self-sufficiency.

Finishing school meant that I now had to deal with bureaucracy: applying for visas, taking out health insurance and paying taxes. The city of Philadelphia has its own tax levy; so, from my meagre earnings, I had to pay exorbitant health-insurance bills, and taxes to the city of Philadelphia, the Commonwealth of Pennsylvania and the federal government. When you perform in places like California, Wisconsin and New York State, they deduct their state taxes and you claim them back during tax season. By then, however, your bank account is already back to zero after paying quarterly taxes. And, when you get lucky enough to get a refund, it's only a portion of what you've already paid the government. Even if you perform overseas in Canada and Europe, including the UK, you can expect the companies to deduct at least 20 per cent tax – and this excludes the other tax obligations I've mentioned.

I have been on the road performing since my debut in Washington, DC, in the autumn of 2014, but it has taken me quite some time to get out of the trundling circle. People may see our performances and assume that we make a lot of money, but what they don't know is that, by the time we cash our cheques, we've had to give away over at least half of what we've earned. The struggle is real, but most of us make our living in the performing arts because we love it and it is our calling. If we could make more money than just enough to pay our bills, it would be very much welcomed.

Because of my work schedule and the fact that I'm away from Philadelphia for months at a time, I only stayed with the boys in our new apartment for a year. Allan graciously offered to let me stay with him and Reid whenever I was in Philadelphia. He made the excellent point that it would be the best solution for me to live with them – that way, I wouldn't have to deal with wasted rent and landlords who didn't allow me to sublet while I was away. With Bill Guerri and Francesca Condeluci at CAMI, and lawyers helping me to obtain permanent residency in the US, I can save up to buy a house once I acquire this.

---

I have had other triumphs in my career, for instance winning many competitions since I have been in the US – including awards from the Opera Index, the Gerda Lissner Foundation, the Giulio Gari Foundation and the Licia Albanese-Puccini Foundation. Now, I am fortunate to make many important role and house debuts.

For all the awards I have received, I am forever grateful. But for me, the moment that stands out the most is when I won the Metropolitan Opera National Council Auditions in 2013. I performed on the same stage as all the opera greats who had performed before me, with a fantastic orchestra led by the brilliant Maestro Marco

Armiliato. When Eric Owens called my name as one of the winners, I was in shock.

That moment, when I looked around and saw a theatre full to capacity (with nearly 4000 people watching and thousands more listening on the radio), knowing that I was the first black African to win that competition, my heart burst with gratitude.

That moment will forever stay with me.

In it, I remembered the video I had watched, back in high school, of Sir Willard White in the role of Die Sprecher in the 1978 production of *Die Zauberflöte* in Glyndebourne. He was the only black lead in the production; it was his performance that had sparked my interest in opera. There, on the Metropolitan Opera stage on 10 March 2013, I had one of the best days of my life.

I am likewise blessed to have performed the title role of Porgy in Gershwin's *Porgy and Bess* at the Glimmerglass Festival in the summer of 2017, in a production directed by Francesca Zambello and conducted by John DeMain, and made my debut with the English National Opera at the Coliseum on the West End. I could not have foreseen that nine years after seeing *The Mask of Zorro* at the Garrick Theatre, I would be back as one of the headliners of the show and receive incredible reviews from distinguished publications like *The Times*, the *Financial Times* and *The Guardian*. Since that day at the Metropolitan Opera, so many important events in my life have unfolded, and I have not looked back.

These are the crowning moments I wished my family could have seen, especially my grandmother. Her memory lingers on, a constant motivation for me to push forward.

As she told me, it is not how it starts that matters, but how it ends.

# Postlude

All our stories are different – determined and influenced by varying circumstances. Other people's childhood stories may not involve an upbringing as dire as mine; other people still may have had it even worse. Through it all, though, we share the same things: determination to follow our dreams, while applying mind over matter when we encounter challenges and difficulties along the way. Singers are all subject to scrutiny, which can be subjective. But this should deter no one from following his or her passions and dreams.

I have a friend who is so despondent from rejection that he has resigned himself to never trying again. I hope I have succeeded, even a little bit, to fire up his motivation. Like all artists, rejection has been my middle name; as someone who has also tried his hand at writing, I have had a taste of literary rejections and their sometimes blunt criticisms. But, I lick my wounds and try again.

If we artists do twenty auditions and get two gigs out of them, Christmas has come early. If we get five, Jesus has come down from heaven, God has quickened the rapture, and we're in the new Jerusalem! But, even when I get nothing, I've learnt to pick myself up, move on, and focus on work and improving my craft.

Who I was in my old life feels like a fictional character in one of my writings; I feel blessed and grateful for all that has happened in my life. I remember, once again, how my family and I prayed every night when I was growing up; I remember my grandmother thanking God for a wonderful day – in the dark, because we couldn't afford electricity, my hungry stomach singing badly written tunes.

I told my struggling friend that now I understand why my grandmother was always grateful. Whenever I complained, or got rejected, she would say, 'Don't worry, my child, that wasn't meant for you. God is saving something special for you. Keep on trying and improving yourself.' I would nod, defeated inside, having no clue what she was talking about; looking back, I see that every time I've received a rejection, two better opportunities have come down the line shortly afterwards.

For me, rejection is an opportunity to improve and ready myself for that other – better – opportunity that God has in store. The key is to keep your hope and the flame of your faith burning, and to be prepared fo any eventuality.

I have always tried to hold two truths in my mind and heart: the first is that we can exert mind over matter. By the force of our will, we can accomplish much; I have tried in this book to give examples of this. And, second, that we depend upon scores of people, known and unknown, for our lives, our sustenance, for all the ways we can discover and develop our talents. I hope I have remembered all the people who have helped me. I could never have survived this odyssey without them.

Profit and fame are not my primary objectives for writing this book. Rather, I want to share my story for the benefit of others. In addition, through writing, I have finally been able to face the buried emotions that have always haunted me. At last, I have forgiven myself and those who have hurt me, or sought to hurt me, in the past. I head into the unknown – as we all do, for who can know the future?

## POSTLUDE

Whatever comes next in this odyssey will not be the first scary bridge I have crossed. I will continue with my singing career, knowing not what the future holds, only that I will take it one day at a time while working on my craft, on becoming the best individual and artist I can be.

Wherever this book will take me, I do not know. But I am glad that I have written it. I hope that whoever takes the time to read it can find some parallels in their own life, and that he or she enjoys accompanying me on this strange odyssey from Zwide to the world stage.

There are more peaks to climb in my life. There are also, I suspect, more deep valleys. But writing this has given me a chance to reflect on where I come from, how far I have travelled, and how beautiful it is where I am right now.

But, work and responsibilities await me. For this, I have the experience, the will and the sheer power I need. And so, I go forward with hope.

# Acknowledgements

This edition and its birth would not have been possible without my good friend and fellow opera singer Suzanne Vinnik-Richards, who loved my first edition but suggested that I work on an update to reflect changing times and thinking. It is through her that I met my publicist, Katlyn Morahan. Katlyn is also passionate about reading and writing and, much like Amanda Edelman had done on the first book, she became my shadow editor and challenged me. Initially, I had thought this edition would just be an update of some parts, but no, Katlyn is persuasive. We started from the top, and it was like writing a second book. Her constant challenges have paid off.

Special thanks to Marlene Fryer, my publisher, for believing in me and my narrative and breathing new life into my book; her team at Penguin Random House: Rashieda Saliem, Ronel Richter-Herbert and Ryan Africa; and my editor, Angela Voges, who has transposed my book and narrative into a coherent structure.

From the AVA, I benefited from the many hours of coaching time and instruction, as well as the production and the performance of the fourteen roles I did there. I am grateful to Peggy Ulrich, who supported me by underwriting my fellowship cheques every academic month so that I could pay my rent. Peggy also invited me to her home and supported our performances at the AVA. People like Peggy ensured that we could continue thriving in our business without worrying too much about expenses.

I am also grateful to Kevin McDowell, who helped me with funding and expenses when I could not afford to pay rent for two summers.

For all his protestations in music coaching, Maestro Macatsoris has a good heart for helping in life's challenges, and he and Robert Lyon were very helpful in my personal life when I needed letters of recommendation. I am also thankful to Dr William Stone for having written recommendation letters for me. His support ensured my participation in various singing contests.

In addition, Mr Lyon worked very hard with his team in the capital campaign to attract the sponsors who paid for our education and fellowships. I am also grateful to Val Starr, the Dean of Students, who helped me with visa applications, I-20s, and dealing with immigration officials and Homeland Security.

In times when I was short of cash and needed support, David Lofton and Laurent Philippe always helped me. During my first year, my two colleagues, Luigi Boccia and Mo El Zein, also lent financial support, especially when finances from back home were delayed and I needed cash for daily living expenses. Nelson Hebo, my fellow African immigrant from Angola, who was at the AVA for two years, bailed me out more frequently than I can remember.

I am grateful to Len van Zyl, who introduced me to Allan Schimmel and Reid Reames. They have played a fundamental role in my life, and became two of my biggest cheerleaders, while supporting me in all my writing and singing endeavours. Through Allan, I met Tom Weisgerker, who has continued to be my friend and fan; I am grateful to have met him.

Through my participation in the First Presbyterian Church, I

## ACKNOWLEDGEMENTS

met Robert Cole, aka Bob, a young African-American, eighty-six years of age. When I self-published the first edition of this memoir, Mr Cole underwrote all the costs of the editor, Mary Nielsen of Zion Publishing in Iowa; he, along with Allan and members of the First Presbyterian Church in Philadelphia, hosted my first book launch. I was fortunate to have had a second launch in Mr Cole's private residence.

Mr Cole resembles my great-grandfather in so many ways: a strong and educated black man, focused on doing good for the community. I'm so grateful that he is part of my life.

I will forever be grateful to Professor Virginia Davids, her husband John and the members of the ComArt organisation for their unwavering support and love. They made Cape Town a warm hearth to dwell upon, even amid all of life's challenges.

I am grateful to Bill Guerri, my manager, and his assistant, Francesca Condeluci, who have been a joy to work with.

There are myriad people to thank. So, to everyone who has played a fundamental role in my life, I thank you from the bottom of my heart.